Cambridge Elements

Elements in Religion in Late Antiquity
edited by
Andrew S. Jacobs
Harvard Divinity School

MAGIC AND HERESY IN ANCIENT CHRISTIAN LITERATURE

Shaily Shashikant Patel
Virginia Tech

Shaftesbury Road, Cambridge CB2 8EA, United Kingdom

One Liberty Plaza, 20th Floor, New York, NY 10006, USA

477 Williamstown Road, Port Melbourne, VIC 3207, Australia

314–321, 3rd Floor, Plot 3, Splendor Forum, Jasola District Centre, New Delhi – 110025, India

103 Penang Road, #05–06/07, Visioncrest Commercial, Singapore 238467

Cambridge University Press is part of Cambridge University Press & Assessment, a department of the University of Cambridge.

We share the University's mission to contribute to society through the pursuit of education, learning and research at the highest international levels of excellence.

www.cambridge.org
Information on this title: www.cambridge.org/9781009598415

DOI: 10.1017/9781009331654

© Shaily Shashikant Patel 2025

This publication is in copyright. Subject to statutory exception and to the provisions of relevant collective licensing agreements, no reproduction of any part may take place without the written permission of Cambridge University Press & Assessment.

When citing this work, please include a reference to the DOI 10.1017/9781009331654

First published 2025

A catalogue record for this publication is available from the British Library

ISBN 978-1-009-59841-5 Hardback
ISBN 978-1-009-33166-1 Paperback
ISSN 2633-8602 (online)
ISSN 2633-8599 (print)

Cambridge University Press & Assessment has no responsibility for the persistence or accuracy of URLs for external or third-party internet websites referred to in this publication and does not guarantee that any content on such websites is, or will remain, accurate or appropriate.

For EU product safety concerns, contact us at Calle de José Abascal, 56, 1°, 28003 Madrid, Spain, or email eugpsr@cambridge.org

Magic and Heresy in Ancient Christian Literature

Elements in Religion in Late Antiquity

DOI: 10.1017/9781009331654
First published online: June 2025

Shaily Shashikant Patel
Virginia Tech

Author for correspondence: Shaily Shashikant Patel, shailyp@vt.edu

Abstract: *Magic and Heresy in Ancient Christian Literature* is a genealogical study of two parallel but not coequal discursive trajectories: of "magic" and of "heresy." This longue durée analysis charts how these two discursive streams intersect in myriad ways, for myriad ends, across the first four centuries of selected Christian literature. *Magic and Heresy* attempts to answer in part the question: When and how did early Christian authors start thinking of magic as heresy – that is, as a religious and epistemic system wholly external to their own orthodoxies? Prompted by metacritical concerns about the relationship between magic and heresy, as well as these categories' roles in erecting and maintaining Christian empire, this Element seeks to disrupt tidy conceptual conflations of magic-heresy constructed by ancient authors and replicated in some modern scholarship. *Magic and Heresy* excavates the cycles of discursive disciplining that eventually resulted in these very conflations.

Keywords: early Christianity, ancient magic, late antiquity, ancient Mediterranean religions, heresiology

© Shaily Shashikant Patel 2025

ISBNs: 9781009598415 (HB), 9781009331661 (PB), 9781009331654 (OC)
ISSNs: 2633-8602 (online), 2633-8599 (print)

Contents

Introduction: Imperial Orthodoxy and Its Enduring Épistémè – Toward an Undisciplined Historiography   1

From Christ-Beliefs to Christianity: The First Century   14

The Long Shadow of Emergent Heresiology: The Second Century   24

Between Ascendant Orthodoxy and Empire: The Third Century   35

Totalizing Epistemologies and Imperial Orthodoxy: The Fourth Century   46

Coda: Orthodoxies, Empires, and an Épistémè   56

References   62

Introduction: Imperial Orthodoxy and Its Enduring Épistémè – Toward an Undisciplined Historiography

Readers beware: The title of this Element is deceptive. On its surface, it claims to excavate how the concepts of magic and heresy shifted in meaning across the first four centuries of Christian literature. But when we consider the historical ramifications of how these categories were leveraged, then it becomes clear that this project is about the construction of Christian empire.[1] Christian writers, especially those of the second and third centuries CE, (re)defined "magic" and "heresy" in increasingly narrow ways that "disciplined" these categories such that they became conceptual foils for Christian authors' respective orthodoxies. In late antiquity, successive cycles of discursive disciplining helped erect and maintain imperial orthodoxy, that is, the form of Christianity that eventually became the religion of the Roman Empire in 380 CE. This centuries-long process resulting in imperial orthodoxy was not without casualties. Both magic and heresy were eventually stripped of their vast and dynamic ranges of meaning and sharpened into rhetorical weapons, meaning they were often used to delegitimate, misrepresent, and erase competing religious and epistemic systems.[2] Decolonial scholars call such a destruction of localized knowledges "epistemicide."[3] So, perhaps a more precise (though inelegant) title for this Element might be: "How early Christians discursively disciplined the concepts of magic and heresy across centuries of literature, and how epistemicide engendered by these disciplinary discourses paved the way for late ancient imperial orthodoxy to coalesce."

Magic and Heresy in Ancient Christian Literature shows how stabilizing and then conflating discourses of magic and heresy ultimately helped legitimate and later sustain the Christianized Roman Empire.[4] Not only do these concepts redefine what religious and epistemic systems form imperial orthodoxy, but their roles as disciplinary discourses also had real-world effects.[5] Beyond late antiquity, many European authorities appealed to the conflation magic-heresy in order to justify impositions of imperial or religious power. We can see how this

---

[1] On the discursive construction of empire(s): Bhabha, 2004, esp. pp. 94–120. Especially pertinent for this Element is Bhabha's analysis of imperial reliance on "fixity," which "... connotes rigidity and an unchanging order as well as disorder, degeneracy, and daemonic repetition" (94).

[2] On Roman religion as an epistemic system: Ando, 2008, pp. 1–20. Here, I refer to a wide range of beliefs and practices as "epistemic systems" – from Greco-Roman philosophies, to magic, to Christianities. Since Christian authors malign "heresies" as bad knowledge, "religious and epistemic systems" works as a conceptual shorthand for all the ways ancient people acquired and disseminated knowledge of the gods and how to worship them. On the applicability of "religion" to the ancient context, including caveats: see Nongbri, 2013, pp. 44–64.

[3] Padilla Peralta, 2020; citing de Sousa Santos, 2014, p. 18.

[4] On the "Christianization" of Rome: MacMullen, 1984. [5] Cameron, 2008, esp. pp. 112–113.

works if we conduct a very brief reception history of one of the most influential works in Western literature, Augustine of Hippo's (d. 430 CE) *City of God Against the Pagans*. This treatise is ostensibly directed at aristocratic pagans who blamed Christianity for the sack of Rome in 410 CE.[6] Some pagans argued that the new ascendant religion had not protected the Eternal City because it promoted the worship of a God who valorizes submission.[7] In his bid to redirect such accusations and turn them against his detractors, Augustine makes a series of rather bold claims. He argues that Rome's long-standing civic religion is to blame for the attack. Roman paganism is tantamount to demonolatry. In fact, paganism and all other heresies are driven by magic, which is also demonic. These assertions rest on a conflation of magic and heresy by way of their inherent demonism. By late antiquity, "magic-heresy" is commonplace, so Augustine's conflation appears self-evident and stable in *City of God*.[8] But the two categories had a diffuse and shifting range of meanings in the centuries before. Indeed, *City of God* exemplifies the rhetorical sleights-of-hand needed to create and maintain a stable magic-heresy conflation. In the first move, Augustine filters the whole cosmos through a totalizing binary; he posits two realms of existence that correspond to his own notions of orthodoxy and heresy. Then, he leverages the notion of magic-heresy to dismiss all competing religious and epistemic systems as demonolatrous error – as an intentional choice heretics make in order to corrupt the truth.

City of God's totalizing cosmology is particularly illustrative because it shows us how Augustine restricts the sorts of meaning an audience makes, of his treatise, sure, but also of the world around them. To put it in Foucaultian terms: Augustine arranges all religious and epistemic systems that have existed or will ever exist into a decidedly Christian épistémè.[9] "Épistémè" is a key term that appears throughout this Element. We can think of an épistémè as governing all discursive possibilities for a time period.[10] It consists of all potential knowledge in a given era, transmitted in cultural codes that facilitate meaning-making through perception, language, relationships, societal hierarchies, and so on.[11] Culturally specific meanings arise because discourses are bounded by an épistémè, one that places limits on meaning-making. This is why some discourses make sense in a given time or place, but not in others.[12] Foucault further claimed that an épistémè is produced unconsciously. Underlying cultural codes

---

[6] On the multiple "falls" of the Roman Empire and their problematic legacies: Watts, 2021.
[7] Discussion in Dyson, 1998, pp. xi–xii.
[8] Kahlos, 2020, discusses this "magicless" Christianity.
[9] This "totalizing" discourse is a hallmark of late ancient heresiology: Cameron, 1994, p. 87; Jacobs, 2004, pp. 21–54.
[10] Foucault, 1970, p. xxii.   [11] Foucault, 1970, p. xx.   [12] Foucault, 1970, p. xxii.

are not necessarily identifiable or understood by people participating in an épistémè's discourses.[13] That said, I want to bracket the question of conscious or unconscious production since we are analyzing ancient, fragmentary evidence. It would be difficult indeed to measure ancient consciousness.

Less difficult, though, is discerning how Augustine's use of earlier and contemporaneous discourses is limited by and further limits possible meanings an audience might make. When *City of God* reduces all history into a cosmic binary, it uses preexisting ideas about what constitutes magic, heresy, and demonolatry. In this way, the text is bounded by the epistemic limits of Christian late antiquity. But *City of God* also articulates new epistemic limits. I think of Augustine and his late ancient counterparts as creating a distinctively Christian épistémè; theirs is a bounded meaning-making arena, or playing field, where the only intelligible discourses are Christian ones. To me, this is why Foucault's notion of the épistémè is useful for the present project. Foucault gives us an intellectual shorthand to name the complex of underlying values and assumptions ancient authors used to construct their own orthodoxies, and simultaneously, to exclude competing understandings of ancient religious and epistemic systems. If an épistémè both facilitates and limits discursive possibility, then *Magic and Heresy in Ancient Christian Literature* shows how such discursive disciplining of magic and heresy became the intellectual anchor for late antiquity's distinctively Christian épistémè, namely by reinforcing some meanings while dismissing others.

Foucault's more abstract theoretical assertion gains clarity if we look at the text of *City of God*. Here, we can detail how Augustine combines earlier discourses and innovates new ones, all with the net result of creating epistemic limits. Consider in more detail Augustine's blanket claim about Roman paganisms. He says pagan gods are angels-turned-demons who do not glorify the true God, but instead seek self-glorification by tricking humans into worshipping them (2.4; 8.22–25). To advance their fraudulent aims, these demons sometimes wear the guise of traditional pagan gods (2.4). But Augustine insists: Roman pagans do not worship real gods, only "malignant spirits" (*maligni spiritus*) or, more simply, "demons" (*daemones*) (2.29). Romans have been worshipping demons since their civic religion was established by the legendary king Numa (7.34–35). *City of God* thus divides the entire cosmos into two tidy halves, represented metaphorically by the "City of God" (i.e., orthodoxy) and the "earthly city" (i.e., heresy). The former realm is defined by love of the true God; the latter by love of self, carnality, and demonolatry (14.3). The two are

---

[13] Foucault, 1970, pp. xx–xxii.

fundamentally and essentially distinct. Such a rigid binary leaves no room for understanding any religious or epistemic system outside notions of Christian orthodoxy and heresy – even if said system predates Christianity.[14] Roman paganisms must be understood as heresy, and as decidedly *Christian* heresy, since Roman gods are corrupted angels-turned-demons and cannot be gods in their own right. *City of God* limits meaning-making around religious and epistemic rivals in tension with its own orthodoxy. These systems are heresies; there is no room to interpret them as anything else.

City of God also reinforces discursive limits for magic, which, like heresy, belongs to the earthly city. Augustine claims, "all the miracles of magicians … operate through the teachings and deeds of demons" (*omnia miracula magorum … doctrinis fiunt et operibus daemonum*: 8.19).[15] So when marvels appear in pagan temples, they must be resultant of human trickery or magic (*magia*), with magic being a product of demonic collusion (21.6). Christian miracles, on the other hand, are driven by God, who works them through the help of angels (10.8). Miracle and magic differ in quality and effect, too: Miracle is far more impressive (21.6) and it has the added benefit of freeing humans from demons' magical misdeeds (7.33–5; 9.15). In *City of God*'s épistémè, magic cannot be Christian.[16] It is external to Christianity; it is heresy. Elsewhere, Augustine even describes Roman paganisms as "public magic" that was rightfully abolished when Christianity became the imperial religion (*magica publica*, at *sermo* 62.28 [Dolbeau]).[17] Magic is heresy; Augustine leaves no room to interpret it as anything else.

City of God's paradoxically totalizing and reductive rhetoric means any religious or epistemic system must be understood as Christian orthodoxy *or* demonolatrous magical heresy. So, if we wish to apprehend a form of paganism – say, Isis worship – then it can only be seen and described as demonic magic-heresy.[18] This narrow view of ancient religiosity may appear patently incorrect to historians of ancient Mediterranean religions and philosophies. We know that other religious and epistemic systems existed and that these systems did not self-define as Christian heresies. And yet, I would argue that texts like *City of God* were very successful in delimiting how later Western European thinkers understood and framed diverse religious and ritual phenomena. Augustine's claim that Roman

---

[14] For example, the relegation of Babylon, Assyria, and pre-Christian Rome to the "Earthly City." See discussion in Dyson, 1998, p. xx.
[15] LCL 413, p. 88.
[16] See, too, Augustine's defense of Christianity against accusations of magic: *cons. ev.* 1.10.15; *contra Faust.* 29; discussion and evidence in Kahlos, 2019, p. 198, n. 20.
[17] Kahlos, 2015, pp. 165–166.
[18] Augustine is not the only late ancient writer to posit a totalizing cosmology. See Jacobs, 2021, p. 81 (citing Schott, 2007 and Kim, 2006, esp. pp. 179–195) for Epiphanius' totalizing view. On late ancient reconfigurations of history more broadly: Cameron, 1994, pp. 120–154.

pagans worship evil angels-turned-demons demands that modern analysts of ancient Christianity neglect rather a lot of Greco-Roman demonology. Demons could be any or all of the following: intermediary divinities who might bring good or evil to humans; life-long companions who advocated for a soul after death; and yes, as a source of magical powers.[19] But within the intellectual arena created by *City of God*, a demon is only intelligible as an evil entity opposed to the only true God. In other words, Augustine's totalizing and rigidly binary cosmology requires eliding Roman paganisms' own polyvalent demonology. Accepting *City of God's* central premise entails epistemicide.

City of God's reception among Western European religious and state authorities shows how this sort of epistemicide continues beyond late antiquity with devastating real-world consequences. In the tenth-century CE, this late ancient conflation of magic-heresy appears in the *Canon Episcopi*, an ecclesiastical rule for instructing clergy. Clergy are told to rid paganism from the women in their congregations, since women mistakenly believe they worship Diana but worship demons instead.[20] Bishops should eject anyone who uses magical art (*magicam artem*), because magic was invented by the devil (C. 15 q.2 c. 4). The *Canon Episcopi* gains more traction once it becomes integrated into the definitive source for canon law in the European Middle Ages, Gratian's *Decretum* (ca. 1140 CE).[21] Still later, Thomas Aquinas (1225–1274 CE) cites Augustine directly in his series of disquisitions on Catholic theology, *Summa Theologica*. The *Summa* poses a hypothetical question: Is it acceptable to participate in the observances of magic (*arte notoria* at 2.2b. q.96a pr.)? No, says Aquinas: Any knowledge obtained through magical rites is acquired by consorting with demons and is therefore unlawful (2.2b. q.96a 1 co.).[22] Perhaps the most notorious entry in this reception history is the *Malleus Maleficarum*, a handbook for identifying and prosecuting supposed witches.[23] Initially drafted in 1486 CE by the Dominican inquisitor Henry Insistoris, the *Malleus* integrates all of these religious writings to argue that witchcraft is heresy. In fact, witches are worse than other heretics because they willfully collude with demons (1.1). The *Malleus* was so infamous for its hypersexualized misogyny

---

[19] On demons as good or evil intermediaries: Plutarch, *De def. or.* 415a–d, 417b; as companions and posthumous advocates: Plato, *Phd.* 107d–e; cf., *Rep.* 617d–e, 620d–e; as sources for magic: Apuleius, *Apol.* 43.2; cf., *De deo Soc.* 6–7. Additional examples in Cotter, 1999, pp. 76–83. For fuller discussions of Christian (re)configurations of extant demonological discourses: Brakke, 2006, pp. 213–239, and Proctor, 2022.

[20] Stephens, 2020, pp. 86–87.   [21] Stephens, 2020, p. 88.

[22] Aquinas cites *De Divin. Daem.* 3.4 here; *De Doctr.* 2.20 at 2.2b q.96 a.1 s. c.; and *De Doctr.* 2.23 at 2.2b. q.96 a.1 co.

[23] See references in Broedel, 2003, pp. 40–43.

and advocacy of torture that even other inquisitors were horrified.[24] Despite its critics, it was later put to use by courts during the European Renaissance.[25]

Though brief, this reception history of one influential Christian text shows how the conflation of magic-heresy creates an épistémè that facilitates certain discourses by excluding others. Instructions on how to administer religious law, distillations of Catholic theology, and guidelines for identifying and prosecuting suspected witches use notions of magic-heresy to advance their aims. Conversely, though, we cannot think of magic or heresy except in terms of their conceptual distance from our authors' orthodoxies. Diana worship is always magical and demonolatrous. Individual magical practices necessarily entail demonic collusion and are never innocent. Witchcraft is an arch-heresy that so threatens the Church that it must be violently rooted out and destroyed.

I would not claim that Augustine is directly at fault for the violences of medieval and early modern European witch hunts. The conflation of magic-heresy he wields so well against his pagan opponents is not unique to him. It appears often in late ancient Christian writings. In the final fourth-century redaction of the Pseudo-Clementine *Homilies*, all heresies originate in the knowledge of magic (8.13–14).[26] Around the same time, Epiphanius' (d. 403 CE) *Panarion* makes magic into a precursor to heresy; it is the ungodly raw material from which heresies emerge (1.1.4). John Chrysostom (d. 407 CE) claims solicitous women ensnare good Christian men with magical spells, resulting in apostasy and condemnation (*Hom. 1 Cor. 7.2–4*).[27] On the whole, late ancient writers accept the view that magic is heresy, or, at least, that magic engenders heresy.[28] These writers are trapped within and help fortify the distinctively Christian épistémè that I will argue coalesces during their time. This new epistemic regime, adopted and refined by Augustine, and presumed by his later interpreters, even limits how we moderns understand magic, heresy, and the relationship between the two categories. The violent legacy of magic-heresy did not end with the Renaissance. Later European empires justified their geopolitical domination by arguing that colonized peoples practiced magic and were not sufficiently "religious" as a result.[29] European intellectuals of the Enlightenment and post-Enlightenment period continued viewing magic as heresy, and used this conflation as a foil for correct Protestant piety.[30] Even

---

[24] Brauner, 2001, pp. 48–49.   [25] Broedel, 2003, p. 3.
[26] *Hom.* 8.13–14. I cannot responsibly address the gendered notion of magic here and in Chrysostom. For the latter: Mitchell, 2022. See also: Stratton, 2007; Stratton and Kalleres, 2014, particularly the essay by Reed, 2014.
[27] PG 5.51.216; discussion in Mitchell, 2022.
[28] Flint, 1999, pp. 324–347; Kahlos, 2015, pp. 167–170.   [29] Chidester, 2014, pp. 159–170.
[30] Styers, 2008, pp. 69–120.

modern scholars of earliest Christianity sometimes find ourselves trapped in the powerful and resonant Christian épistémè created among late ancient *literati*.

One result of what I am calling the late ancient épistémè is the fixity it imparts. We are left with the impression that magic was always viewed as heresy, that it was always an evil and demonic other to Christianity. But as the following sections will show, these two concepts had their own discursive trajectories. They were not always seen as coequal, not even in formative *Christian* literature. In so many ways, this Element was prompted by the conceptual disjuncture between how we see magic and heresy being used in the earliest Christian texts and how they later come to be used by Augustine and his contemporaries. This project is an intellectual experiment aimed at answering a deceptively simple question: How did Christian writers discursively discipline these profoundly unruly categories so that magic became coequal with heresy, and conversely, so that heresy necessarily implicated magic?

The question is worth asking precisely because this conflation of magic-heresy is unintelligible when we take into account how both terms were used in earlier and wider literary circles. Our evidence suggests that ancient magic was a massive category with a broad and sometimes conflicting range of meanings.[31] Contrary to the definition of magic we see most often in scholarship on earliest Christianity, it was not primarily used for what we might call "religious othering" until the second-century CE at the earliest.[32] Beyond this particular use, magic was deployed to orientalize foreign practitioners; mark specific deeds as frivolous or deceptive; relegate something to a culture's "primitive" past; reify gender norms, and much more.[33] We even have evidence that some people self-labeled as magicians or admitted to using magic.[34] Heresy, too, was a similarly complicated category. For much of Greco-Roman antiquity, it referred to philosophical positions and meant something like "intellectual trajectory."[35] This category also took on a disciplining role in the second-century CE. Before then, heresy had mostly neutral connotations.[36] Over several hundred years, the diffuse discursive lineages of both magic and heresy get collapsed until we have fairly stable conceptual binaries like the ones that give *City of God* so much rhetorical leverage: orthodoxy versus heresy, divine versus demonic, miracle versus magic, and good versus evil.

---

[31] Such complexity is reflected in the works of: Dickie, 2008; Edmonds, 2019; Frankfurter, 2019; Gordon, 1999; Graf, 1997; Stratton, 2007.

[32] This use of magic to police religion coalesced over time: Rives, 2003; Stratton, 2007, pp. 107–141.

[33] On the first three: Gordon, 1999, pp. 191–243. On gendering: Stratton, 2007, pp. 12–14; the essays in Stratton and Kalleres, 2014. On many other uses of magic: the essays in Frankfurter, 2019.

[34] For example, PGM 1.331, IV.210, IV.244, where experts performing the prescribed rites are assumed to be magic-users. See, too, Edmonds, 2019, pp. 396–401.

[35] Simon, 1979, p. 109; Le Boulluec, 2022, pp. 16–17.   [36] Le Boulluec, 2022, pp. 14–15.

Modern scholars of earliest Christianity are not immune to our sources' presuppositions about magic and heresy. Sometimes we seem to be trapped in the épistémè assumed and advanced by Augustine and Aquinas, meaning that we impose a late ancient (or later) view of magic-heresy on earlier evidence. This makes it difficult to understand ancient magic and heresy apart from their conceptual distance to earliest Christianity, or our scholarly reconstructions of it, at any rate. This tendency is most visible to me in scholarly frameworks for ancient magic offered by those working in the subfield of early Christianity. Scholars in other subfields have long acknowledged the polyvalency of magic, but we very often reduce magic to a pejorative label marking religious deviance and theological outsiders.[37] In other words, we assume one person's magic was another's miracle. This was certainly one way of using magic – and one we see frequently among Christian writers. But such a scholarly framework can also obscure; applying it to ancient evidence means we only see magic when it stands in tension with early Christianity.[38]

Let me explain. One popular framework for ancient magic comes from Susan R. Garrett's groundbreaking 1989 monograph, *The Demise of the Devil: Magic and the Demonic in Luke's Writings*. In this book, Garrett criticizes earlier historians who first craft their own definitions of ancient magic and then proceed to identify magic among ancient evidence. These approaches were problematic because ultimately, scholars presupposed the definitions for magic that they purported to prove. Moving beyond essentialist approaches, Garrett instead frames magic as a "locative or relational category" that marks difference between an individual and those they wish to discredit.[39] Garrett's framework is among one of the most nuanced in the study of early Christian literature. She rightfully states that concepts like magic cannot have stable meanings, because meanings are negotiated in context.[40] But even this sophisticated analytic demands we assume the existence of a very early and cohesive religion – a Christianity – against which we identify ancient magic.[41] It demands we play by the rules of *City of God's* épistémè and define magic by its conceptual distance from orthodoxy. Take scholarly commentary on Acts 19:13–16, the story of the Sons of Scaeva. The pericope reads as follows:

> (13) Now some itinerant Jewish exorcists (ἐξορκιστῶν) attempted to call the name of the Lord Jesus upon those having evil spirits, saying, "I adjure you by Jesus whom Paul preaches." (14) They were seven sons of a certain Scaeva, a Jewish high priest, who were doing this. (15) Answering, the evil spirit said

---

[37] Select examples include: Garrett, 1989; Holmén, 2007; Janowitz, 2001; Klauck, 2003; Porter, 2007; Ricks, 1995; Twelftree, 2020; Witmer, 2012.
[38] Review of scholarship in Patel, 2021.   [39] Garrett, 1989, pp. 4–5.
[40] Garrett, 1989, pp. 4–5.   [41] Patel, 2021.

to them, "Jesus I know, and I recognize Paul. But who are you?" (16) Then, the man who had the evil spirit leaped upon them, and overpowered them all, dominating them so they fled from that house naked and wounded.[42]

Some scholars of early Christian literature read this passage as a blanket indictment of magic.[43] Garrett herself claims that Luke depicts the Sons of Scaeva as mistaking Paul's wonders for magic.[44] They try to usurp Paul's authority by exorcising demons in his name. But because the Sons are magic-users, Luke describes them as emissaries of Satan. This is why they cannot access the same divine power as Paul. When Luke maligns the Sons of Scaeva, he makes and marks difference between these Jewish magicians and Paul, a Christian miracle worker. Acts 19:13–16 shows that "... Christians have never sided with magic, and therefore with Satan."[45]

I think reading Acts 19:13–16 in a rigidly anti-magic way necessitates sleights-of-hand similar to those we saw in *City of God*. This interpretation filters rituals like exorcism through totalizing and reductive binaries of insider versus outsider, miracle versus magic, and (proto-)orthodoxy versus heresy.[46] In Garrett's paradigm, the Sons' failed exorcism must be understood as satanic magic since it very clearly is not Christian miracle. Alternative readings are impossible because magic is, by definition, the purview of Christianity's theological enemies. But what if magic has nothing to do with the Sons' plight? What if we only see anti-magic invective because we are so used to viewing magic as heresy? Luke-Acts itself troubles Garrett's assertion that Christians never sided with magic. For one, the Greek μαγεία and close cognates do not appear in or near Acts 19:13–16.[47] The Sons of Scaeva are called "exorcists" (ἐξορκιστῶν, at 19:13). In fairness, exorcism *was* commonly associated with magic, but this is insufficient for reading the failed exorcism at Acts 19:13 as broad anti-magic invective. If maligning magic were Luke's primary goal, then why not use the Greek μαγεία? He uses it against competing ritual experts elsewhere (Acts 8:9–24 and 13:6–12). Moreover, Luke has a very intricate view of exorcism. In the Gospel (9:49–50), Jesus refuses to exclude exorcists who "[do] not follow with us," but who nevertheless cast out demons in his name. He says, "Do not stop [them]. For whoever is not against us is with us" (9:50). Then, in the Beelzebul Controversy (Luke 11:14–23), Jesus defends his own

---

[42] Text from the NA28. Translations my own unless noted otherwise.
[43] Examples include: Conzelmann, 1988, p. 163; Fitzmyer, 1988, p. 646; Garrett, 1989, pp. 90–99; Klauck, 2003, p. 100; Stenschke, 1999, pp. 133–143. Criticism of this reading in Sanzo, 2019, pp. 202–209.
[44] The following summarized from Garrett, 1989, pp. 90–104.   [45] Garrett, 1989, p. 104.
[46] "Proto-orthodoxy" is a conceptual placeholder to describe the form of Christianity that later becomes imperial orthodoxy.
[47] Following Sanzo, 2019, p. 206.

exorcistic legitimacy by claiming he works through the same divine power as other successful Jewish exorcists (11:19–20).

Luke's Jesus Movement and Jewish exorcists are on the same side in the Gospel, but the latter can no longer access divine power in Acts. Garrett is certainly correct when she claims that Acts 19:13–16 makes the Sons of Scaeva outsiders. But we should not assume that outsider status to Acts' Jesus Movement means these ritual experts are supposed to be seen as magicians, or indeed that all who dabble in magic are outsiders. We need not accept our authors' premise that Christianity and magic were always at odds. If we escape the magic versus early Christianity binary, we might ask a more interesting set of questions, ones recognizing the polyvalency of contemporaneous discourses of ancient magic: Why, precisely, do the Sons of Scaeva deserve this rebuke? What prevents them from accessing the divine power successfully used by Jewish exorcists in Luke 11:19–20? Upon closer read, it appears likely that Luke wishes to restrict legitimate exorcistic authority to those deputized by Christ as his emissaries on earth (Luke 9:1, 10:19; Acts 1:4–5, 9). In Acts 19:13, Luke explicitly highlights the Sons' Jewishness, placing them among those the author blames for Jesus' crucifixion (3:13–15). Luke never uses μαγεία to describe exorcisms. And those he describes as magic-users never perform exorcisms. In fact, Luke has a special role for exorcism, which is uniquely suited to signifying the inbreaking of the Kingdom of God.[48] Taken together, this evidence suggests a different reading of Acts 19:13–16. Yes, the pericope "others" the Sons of Scaeva, but not because they were magicians.[49] They transgress because they try to usurp divine power, which must now be limited to Luke's protagonists. Acts' message is clear: After Christ's ascension, Jewish exorcists can no longer access divine power. This explanation fits Acts 19:13–16 better than rigidly anti-magic interpretations. It also allows us to detect Luke's relatively positive, or at least neutral, view of exorcism – a magical practice insofar as it was stereotypically associated with magic in wider Greco-Roman literature.[50] When read this way, Luke-Acts is not flatly anti-magic. And although their texts distance Christianity from magic, ancient authors like Luke clearly did not relegate *all* magic to outsider heretics.[51] Ancient Christian literature is littered with the magical, its influence most clear where it is most vehemently denied.

---

[48] Twelftree, 2007, p. 132–134. [49] Sanzo, 2019, p. 206.
[50] For example, Lucian, *Philop.* 16; Celsus, in Origen, *C. Cels.* 1.68; Irenaeus, *Adv. Haer.* 2.31.1–2, implicated when Irenaeus claims non-Christian exorcisms are "magical illusions."
[51] I devote a forthcoming monograph to this subject: *Smoke & Mirrors: Discourses of Magic in Early Petrine Traditions* (2025).

These subtle literary negotiations around magic, (proto-)orthodoxy, and heresy require more flexible methodologies that can capture shifts in critical categories. Fortunately, there exists an impressive and innovative pool of scholarship on ancient magic.[52] We scholars of early Christianity could better integrate these field-adjacent and interdisciplinary approaches, but such a task is beyond the scope of this Element. Instead of articulating a specific paradigm for studying ancient heresy or magic, I dispense with definitions altogether and instead trace discursive shifts in both categories across the first four centuries of Christian literature. *Magic and Heresy* is best approached as a reference work for fuller studies or further methodological innovation. The following sections detail how magic and heresy were combined via emphasis on demonolatry as well as how this conflation reached relative stability prior to Christianity becoming Roman imperial religion. Once stable, magic-heresy offers a compelling and powerful way to make and mark religious deviance. In the end, if magic and heresy were gradually disciplined to become rhetorical weapons, then the present project represents an "undisciplining," one that attempts to unravel such a tidy and powerful conflation.

Methodology and Structure

I describe *Magic and Heresy in Ancient Christian Literature* as a genealogical survey of early Christian literature, but even a genealogy needs a starting point. If I want to measure change over time, I should establish a conceptual "control" to follow across the evidence. My control consists of two pairs of Greek and Latin terms: αἵρεσις/*haeresis* and μαγεία/*magia*. These terms anchor the ensuing longue durée study. I start with an overview of heresy and magic in first-century CE Christian literature and each section covers roughly a century of evidence. I end with the fourth-century CE, when ruling views of magic-heresy helped establish and maintain Christianity as the religious epicenter of the Roman Empire. This sort of organizational schema is an expedient and not intended as a firm declaration about dating specific texts. I default to the most commonly accepted dates. More important, to me, is the core aim of analyzing discursive shifts and locating them within broader cultural and literary trends. In order to clearly present these shifts, I divide every section into parts: one dedicated to the construction of heresy, another to magic, a "case study" that highlights how the two categories come together (or not), and finally, an integrative coda contextualizing discursive developments over the century in question. Finally, I circumscribe this Element by focusing on imperial

---

[52] Select works include Dickie, 2008; Edmonds, 2019; Gordon, 1999; the essays in Frankfurter, 2019.

orthodoxy and its literary "ancestors." While the texts in the following pages are not exclusively limited to proto-orthodox texts, I choose exemplars that allow us to see the discursive scaffolding that will anticipate the magic-heresy conflation of late antiquity. A narrow study like this one can never account for all the nuances in categories as contested as heresy or magic. Albeit lacunose, and perhaps a little disorderly, this survey exposes instead the rhetorical moves early Christian authors made toward disciplining and stabilizing two unwieldy concepts.

In the first-century CE, heresy and magic are used in diverging ways and do not refer to the same phenomena. Early canonical texts link μαγεία with ritual expertise and use it in negotiations of apostolic authority. First century uses of αἵρεσις also make and mark difference, particularly between authors' orthodoxies and Judaism. These early moves begin the process of distinguishing the Jesus Movement from magicians and heretics but in diverging ways. From Christ-Beliefs to Christianity: The First Century's case study is the canonical Acts. Magic and heresy do not meet in Acts. This is unsurprising since neither the Jesus Movement nor those deemed outsiders were clearly defined. Magic and heresy do meet in the second century, though. The Long Shadow of Emergent Heresiology: The Second Century surveys independent uses of each term but also highlights the first clear conflation of their discursive lineages, exemplified by Irenaeus of Lyons' (d. ca. 202 CE) *Against Heresies*. Two contemporaneous trends provide the impetus for disciplining heresy and magic: First, Roman legal writings evidence the use of "magic" to police proper *religio*, initially in an ad hoc fashion, but later in a more generalizing way.[53] Second, this period witnesses the emergence of Christian heresiology as a distinct literary genre. Heresiologists link magic to heresy by way of ritual expertise much like earlier texts. In the case study, Irenaeus introduces the dreaded magician-heresiarch figure, a character that will haunt subsequent writings, too. This individual is most often depicted as a depraved usurper who deceives followers with demonic magic. Magician-heresiarchs recede in the third-century CE, though they always linger, especially in the literary lives and afterlives of Simon of Samaria. The many "crises" of this era betray authorial anxieties around Christianity's increasing visibility within the broader matrix of Roman religious and epistemic systems. Its new fame precipitated accusations of magic against Christianity. And Christian communities experienced brief periods of persecution by Roman authorities. The anti-magic rhetoric of these texts responds to a rapidly evolving historical situation that necessitates stronger rhetorical weapons. Between Ascendant Orthodoxy and

---

[53] Rives, 2003.

Empire: The Third Century's case study, the *Refutation against all the Heresies* attributed to Hippolytus of Rome (d. ca. 235 CE), exemplifies how reigning concerns prompt an expansion of magic beyond its use in maligning competing ritual experts. Finally, in Totalizing Epistemologies and Imperial Orthodoxy: The Fourth Century, fourth-century *literati* use earlier proto-orthodox notions of magic-heresy to forge the Christian épistémè we saw in Augustine. Conceptual binaries between magic and miracle, heresy and orthodoxy, and error and truth are naturalized – presumed, in other words, and not explained. Authors expand the intellectual domain of magic-heresy to apply to *all* religious and epistemic rivals. In this section, I use some texts modern scholars have labeled as "heterodox" to show how commonplace the conflation of magic-heresy had become. Here, one person's magic becomes another's miracle. This section ends as one might expect – with Eusebius of Caesarea's (d. 339 CE) *Ecclesiastical History*, a conspicuously tidy historiography that imagines Christianity's past persecutions as presaging its destiny at the epicenter of empire. Eusebius works within and further extends a distinctively Christian épistémè which was dependent on totalizing and reductive narratives. And so, this Element ends where it began, in late antiquity's enduring épistémè. A short Coda returns to issues of empire and epistemicide, their relationship made clear only after the preceding genealogical survey. In the end, I argue that the conflation of magic and heresy, long since naturalized, extends empire by perpetuating epistemicide.

My proposed structure requires, I acknowledge, several methodological deficiencies in terms of my approach. Throughout the following pages, I ask that my readers keep them firmly in mind. The first deficiency lies in my almost exclusive dependency on Greek and Latin vocabulary, meaning my results are partial at best. These results are further limited by my focus on these particular terms. Scholars have identified a veritable lexicon associated with μαγεία/*magia*. Some closely related terms include "sorcery" (γοητεία), "potion-making" or "enchantment" (φαρμακεία/*venena*), and the ever-popular "evil-doing" (*maleficium*).[54] But other ancient languages also have terms for phenomena stereotypically associated with what we would translate with the English "magic." Heresy is no less complicated. Its scope can include terms like "heterodoxy" (ἑτεροδοξία), "schism" (σχίσμα/*schisma*), and even "Greeks" (Ἕλληνες). The latter use appears in monastic texts especially, where "Greeks" was a cipher for "pagans," which in turn was tantamount to "heretics."[55] Expansive vocabularies pertaining to ancient heresy and magic only add more uncertainty to the present project. By choosing which terms to include in my genealogies, I have made an implicit claim about

---

[54] Lexical studies of words associated with magic include: Bremmer, 1999; Dombrowski, 2018; Graf, 1997, pp. 20–80; Dickie, 2008. Heresy: Le Boulluec, 2022; Simon, 1979; Royalty, 2015.

[55] Discussion in Schroeder, 2007, pp. 121–129.

what "counts" as magic or heresy. Should this genealogy include φαρμακεία/ *veneficium* as a kind of μαγεία/*magia*? Ought σχίσμα/*schisma* to be considered under the rubric of αἵρεσις/*haeresis*? I do not resolve these problems. That said, I hew very close to μαγεία/*magia* and αἵρεσις/*haeresis*, except on rare occasions where some of the closely related terms mentioned here offer a clearer picture of discursive shifts happening in the original set of Greek and Latin categories. *Magic and Heresy's* brevity necessitates a limited scope, but despite these limitations, we can still gauge how the categories of magic and heresy shift over time. One final methodological caution seems appropriate: I may focus on ancient usage of selected Greek and Latin terms, but the following is not an emic study of ancient magic and heresy. Genealogies cannot be emic, precisely because they assume a scholarly gaze far enough removed from the historical context to detect discursive shifts as well as the broader trends that precipitate said shifts. *Magic and Heresy in Ancient Christian Literature* is as much a scholarly reconstruction as any other historiographical work, and it is therefore rife with all the shortcomings of the genre. Even so, I hope the following conveys the intellectual value of trading tidy conflations of magic-heresy for untidiness, conceptual instability, and some small measure of historiographical chaos.

From Christ-Beliefs to Christianity: The First Century

Alain Le Boulluec's thoroughgoing and masterful study of heresy in second- and third-century CE Greek literature places the advent of heresiology in the second-century CE.[56] By "heresiology," I mean a distinctive literary genre that makes and marks difference among various religious and epistemic systems. In The Long Shadow of Emergent Heresiology: The Second Century, I consider more closely its development. Here, however, I want to take up another of Le Boulluec's assertions: Prior to the emergence of heresiology proper, Christian texts nevertheless produced difference.[57] But these earlier texts seem concerned with enforcing "orthopraxy" more than orthodoxy – that is, they are preoccupied with policing behaviors and practices deemed threats to group cohesion rather than identifying incorrect beliefs or doctrines.[58] Still, Le Boulluec notes, we should be careful. Early Christian articulations of difference are inherently ambiguous. The behaviors and practices authors prescribe and prohibit are undergirded by implicit and oftentimes obscured beliefs.[59] In other words, first-century Christian writings do indeed produce difference based on praxis. When they malign incorrect practices and behaviors, however, they also

---

[56] Le Boulluec, 2022, pp. 57–59.
[57] The following discussion summarized in Le Boulluec, 2002, pp. 2–3. See, too, Royalty, 2015, esp. pp. 3–4.
[58] Le Boulluec, 2002, pp. 2–3.   [59] Le Boulluec, 2002, p. 3.

betray implicit beliefs about Christ. Later heresiology works precisely because it makes explicit the Christ-beliefs implicit in this earlier evidence.[60] Before we can speak of Christianity, or multiple Christianities even, we can detect heresiological discourses in its writings.[61]

So how do the two categories under study – αἵρεσις and μαγεία – help lay the epistemic foundation for the "invention" of Christianity in the second-century CE? This section argues that threats to group cohesion, denoted by the Greek term αἵρεσις, were precipitated by real or perceived differences in belief. Improper belief imperils individuals' adherence to the correct gospel. Magic is used in comparable ways but does not denote the same phenomena as heresy. Overwhelmingly, magic is used to describe ritual experts who are or should be subordinate to the leaders of the Jesus Movement. Canonical narratives about magic-users teach the audience how to view rival religious specialists in comparison with Jesus, Peter, and Paul – namely, these rivals ought to be seen as inferior and/or potentially usurpatious. But in this early evidence, αἵρεσις and μαγεία never appear together as a means of maligning the same individuals or practices, and certainly not as a means of delegitimizing entire religious and epistemic systems. This section's case study, the canonical Acts of the Apostles, does not make magic into heresy, not like Augustine. But Luke does leverage αἵρεσις and μαγεία for a common purpose: To establish leadership hierarchies and to facilitate group cohesion. So begins the long processes of meaning-making and self-definition that become sharper and more robust in later texts, many of which rely on early community norms that Christ-believers were supposed to hold in common. Ultimately, first-century discourses of magic and heresy resulted in two oft-used means of circumscribing orthodoxy in subsequent Christian literature – supersessionism and apostolic succession.

Heresy before Heresiology

In keeping with the roughly chronological approach I outlined in my introduction, I want to survey the earliest uses of αἵρεσις and its derivatives occurring in the canonical epistles. In his letters, written in the middle of the first century, Paul uses the noun αἵρεσις to speak of "schisms," while reserving the verb αἱρέω to impose rigid binaries on the choices adherents can make. Later letters take up this theme, helping to sharpen the contours of heresy by deploying it in much narrower ways than we see in wider Greco-Roman literary circles. In Greek and Roman texts, αἵρεσις and αἱρέω have abstract and neutral connotations. The verb αἱρέω usually means "to take or grasp" or "to choose."[62] The noun αἵρεσις,

---

[60] Le Boulluec, 2002, p. 3.
[61] See Royalty, 2015, who offers a monograph-length study of earliest heresiological discourse.
[62] In the LSJ (Liddell and Scott *Greek-English Lexicon*, 1940). Available online: https://lsj.gr/wiki/αἱρέω.

appropriately, means something like "choice." More often, though, heresy refers to a "course of action or thought," a "sect," or a "faction."[63] Neither word form necessitates a negative evaluation. And yet, by the second-century CE, Church Fathers like Justin Martyr (d. 165 CE) can use αἵρεσις against rival religious and epistemic systems, marking them as evil and demonic. Canonical texts show how the broad, more neutral use of the category shifts into the rigidly pejorative one wielded by Justin and others. The New Testament is therefore a conceptual baseline for subsequent disciplining of heresy; its texts narrow the meaning of αἵρεσις by imbuing it with eschatological significance. As a choice between salvation and condemnation, heresy offers authors a way to legitimate their own gospels while claiming legitimate worship of the Jewish God for Christ-believers.

Our earliest evidence comes from Paul, who uses the verb αἱρέω to describe a choice he made on behalf of his assembly of Christ-believers. He ties this choice to eschatological outcomes, and only two are possible: salvation or condemnation. In Phil. 1:22–23, Paul agonizes over making a choice (αἱρήσομαι, at 1:22) between living for the sake of believers and longing for death. Though death would allow him to be with Christ, he chooses to live so that he might inculcate in his followers "progress and joy in faith" (1:25). Such "progress" is evident when congregants abide in one spirit, one mind, and follow the gospel Paul preaches (1:21). Paul's difficult choice leads to salvation for Christ-believers; in return, they follow his saving gospel. Elsewhere, Paul rails against false teachers and their gospels (Gal 1:6–9). We can guess, therefore, that Paul is concerned with establishing his own authority, which he does by claiming he made a self-sacrificing choice in order to preach a salvific gospel. But he also makes a normative claim about who "counts" as a Christ-believer: those who follow his gospel, ever-abiding in one mind and one spirit.

Later epistles dated between the late first and early second-century CE echo Pauline associations among αἱρέω, salvation, and choice as markers of belonging. God chooses (εἵλατο) the Thessalonians as "first fruits" for salvation in the pseudepigraphal 2 Thessalonians (2:13).[64] Before describing God's choice, the author contrasts the addressed community with others who reject the truth because they have been deceived by the Antichrist (2:9–10). God's chosen are the author's chosen – the Thessalonians – saved because they received "our gospel" (2 Thess. 2:14). In Hebrews, an anonymous letter written between 60–95 CE, we see similar views of heresy as Paul and

---

[63] LSJ: https://lsj.gr/wiki/αἵρεσις.
[64] Dating 2 Thess. is largely dependent on its authorship. If written by Paul, it dates from the 50s CE. More likely, the text is pseudepigraphal, making dating very difficult (Coogan et al., 2001, p. 345 [NT]). I include it in this section because its use of heresy parallels other first-century exemplars.

2 Thessalonians. Hebrews depicts Moses as choosing (ἑλόμενος, at 11:25) to suffer alongside God's people instead of partaking in carnal pleasures. Indeed, Moses is one of many figures from Jewish mythic history whose "faith" persevered in anticipation of the promised resurrection (11:4–40). These early uses of αἱρέω in post-Pauline epistles ossify earlier conceptual links among choosing salvation, adhering to the correct gospel, and belonging to a like-minded community of Christ-believers. We should also note the supersessionism, most evident in Hebrews, which characterizes a legendary Jewish prophet as a Christ-believer. Even if αἱρέω means "to choose" in these texts, its use forces a binary on the choices available. Rival teachings are either a rejection of truth or, at best, a choice to *not* follow the saving gospel. These early moves lay the foundation for a major theme that will reappear in the following sections: Heresy is resultant of a choice made between truth and error, and Christian authors are the arbiters of salvific knowledge.

The noun αἵρεσις appears more often in canonical texts. Like the verb, it also forces a binary choice of eschatological outcomes. In 1 Corinthians 11:18, Paul says he has heard of "schisms" (σχίσματα) within his congregation. These heresies (αἱρέσεις – referring to the schisms in v. 18) exist so that worthy adherents might be identified and acknowledged (11:19). Unworthy followers sow division and bring judgment upon themselves through their indecorous behavior at the Lord's Supper (11:27–29). The notion that fomenting schisms precludes salvation reappears in Gal. 5:20. Αἱρέσεις materialize among "works of the flesh," inclusive of sexual immorality, idolatry, potion-making (φαρμακεία), drunkenness, and so on. We should briefly consider the appearance of φαρμακεία alongside αἱρέσεις in this very early evidence. The NRSVue translates this term as "sorcery," and indeed, the term eventually acquires this broader meaning.[65] But as we saw with Acts 19:13–16, authors can also isolate specific practices associated with magic. In wider Greco-Roman literature, φαρμακεία refers to the preparation of curatives, potions, and poisons.[66] It must be translated in context. In Gal. 5:20, φαρμακεία likely refers to potion-making or poisoning – an activity, like drunkenness or sexual immorality, that can have deleterious effects on the body and soul.[67] Even if we retain the translation of "sorcery," we do not yet have the conceptual overlap between magic and heresy we see in later Christian authors. We can say, however, that using φαρμακεία and fomenting αἱρέσεις prevent one from inheriting the Kingdom of God (5:21). Throughout Gal. 5:1–26, Paul subsumes such fleshly works under an overarching invective against false teachers

---

[65] Stratton, 2007, pp. 26–30.   [66] See the online LSJ: https://lsj.gr/wiki/φαρμακεία.
[67] Rives' discussion of *veneficium* in Roman legal writings offers an intellectual foothold for how poisoning becomes conflated with magic: 2003, pp. 318–320.

who insist salvation depends on adherence to Mosaic Law – an accusation later taken up by the author of 2 Peter, who also claims false teachers secretly bring in αἱρέσεις (2:1).[68] These false teachers will be punished by God (Gal. 5:10 and 2 Pet. 2:1), and anyone following them has separated themselves from Christ (Gal. 5:3 and 2 Pet. 2:2–3). A similar argument can be found in Titus, a pseudepigraphal letter wherein a "heretical man" (αἱρετικὸν ἄνθρωπον, at 3:10) stands self-condemned for fomenting dissent concerning the law (3:9).[69] These texts use αἵρεσις and the adjective αἱρετικὸν to malign dissent within the emerging Jesus Movement, especially around adherence to Mosaic Law. For New Testament authors, heretical schisms arise when people follow unauthorized teachings. Dire eschatological consequences will surely follow all who participate in heresy, both leaders and followers.

Magic before Heresiology

In the Christian canon, μαγεία and its derivatives appear a total of seven times, and only in two texts: the Gospel of Matthew and the Acts of the Apostles (Matt. 2:1, 2:7, 2:16; Acts 8:9, 8:11, 13:6, 13:8).[70] These uses cluster around ritual experts: Matthew's "magi" (Matt. 2:1–11), Simon of Samaria (Acts 8:9–24), and Bar-Jesus (Acts 13:6–12).[71] Matthew and Luke differ on how they evaluate magic-users, but both appear to share a common goal of subordinating rival religious experts to their protagonists.

Since we will consider Acts in the case study, I will limit this discussion to Matthew 2:1–16, the famous pericope featuring magi who visit the newborn Jesus. Scholars typically render μάγοι at 2:1 as "wise men," "astrologers," or "magi."[72] But Matthew uses the same lexeme Luke uses to describe Simon of Samaria (Acts 8:9–24) and Bar-Jesus (Acts 13:6–12) – figures recognized as magicians in English translations. Matthew describes his magicians as coming from "the East" (2:1). They can read and follow the stars (2:2, 9–10), which is how they learn that the "King of the Jews" has been born (2:2). Later, we see these magicians receiving warnings in dreams (2:12). Matthew's magicians appear to be well-respected, if intimidating. Their arrival causes Herod the

---

[68] Dating 2 Peter is difficult, though it was likely composed near the end of the first or the beginning of the second-century CE (Coogan et al., 2001, p. 401 [NT]). I mention its Pauline parallels here, but I will consider its own themes more fully in The Long Shadow of Emergent Heresiology: The Second Century.

[69] Like 2 Thess., Titus' date depends on authorship: Coogan et al., 2001, p. 349 (NT). It too is included in this section for reasons of thematic similarity.

[70] Sanzo, 2019, pp. 202–208.

[71] On freelance experts, and magicians as part of this wider class of practitioners: Wendt, 2016, esp. pp. 114–145.

[72] Sanzo, 2019, p. 203; Vanden Eykel, 2022, pp. 21–25. The NRSVue translates μάγοι as "magi," a departure from the NRSV's "wise men."

Great and the denizens of Jerusalem to become agitated (2:3). Herod arranges a secret meeting to learn when the star portending Jesus' birth appeared (2:7). He then dispatches the magicians to find Jesus (2:7), presumably so he can kill the King of the Jews (2:13).

Matthew 2:1–16 depicts magicians as having expertise, particularly in astrology and dream interpretation – skills we find among other magicians in Greco-Roman literature. In fact, these figures conform to long-standing, orientalized stereotypes of Persian magicians who were thought to be especially adept at astrology and divination (including dream interpretation), and who were sometimes associated with royalty.[73] No doubt Matthew was aware of this stereotype, since 2:1–16 only works if we accept the magicians' expertise. When they prostrate themselves before Christ, for instance, the audience knows they have correctly identified the "King of the Jews" they were looking for (2:2, 11). Moreover, they do not bow to Herod, and disobey him besides (2:12, 16). Matthew 2:1–16 requires a positive evaluation of these magicians precisely because it relies on their expertise – one based on a stereotype of orientalized magic – in order to identify Jesus as king and to elevate him above Herod.

Despite Matthew's text being rooted in what we might call magical expertise, many modern scholars distance these magicians from others in Greco-Roman literature, most visibly by translating μάγοι as something other than "magician." Translation choices betray the underlying presumption that characters who are viewed favorably by early Christian authors cannot be magicians. Yet Matthew 2:1–16 paints a more complicated picture, one leveraging the expertise and renown of magicians to advance a royal Christology. Canonical texts may differ in their respective views of magicians, sure, but magic was a vast and varied discourse.[74] Diverging assessments of it should not lead us to view the magicians in Matthew as fundamentally or essentially different from others who are not evaluated positively.

Case Study: The Acts of the Apostles and the Making of Christianity

Both magic and heresy appear in the canonical Acts. They do not refer to the same phenomena, but both are deployed toward articulating group boundaries and enforcing norms. Luke uses αἵρεσις to center the Jesus Movement as the only legitimate worship of the Jewish God; he uses μαγεία to protect apostolic authority and ministry. Together, these uses represent an early move toward

---

[73] Bremmer, 1999, pp. 4–9. On ancient ethnically coded knowledge: Lampinen, 2022 and Wendt, 2016, pp. 74–113. Tupamahu, 2022, pp. 193–194 discusses ethnic reasoning pertaining to ritually efficacious speech, heteroglossia in particular.

[74] Gordon, 1999, pp. 191–243.

inventing a "Christianity," by which I mean a community of like-minded Christ-believers who worship the Jewish God in prescribed ways and who adhere to group norms.

In Acts, αἵρεσις is a label for various Jewish sects, but it is not neutral. Rather, Luke leverages heresy toward an audaciously supersessionist claim: The Jesus Movement represents the only legitimate worship of the Jewish God. The text explicitly denies that αἵρεσις applies to its new community; at the same time, it labels other Jewish groups as heresies. In Acts 24:1–23, Paul defends himself in court before the Roman governor of Judaea, a man named Felix. Paul's Jewish accusers call him "leader of the heresy (αἱρέσεως) of Nazarenes" (24:5). Later, in 28:22, Paul must again account for the widely-disparaged heresy (αἱρέσεως) to which he belongs. When speaking to Felix in 24:14, Paul says, "according to [the Jesus Movement], which *they* call a heresy (αἵρεσιν), I serve the God of *our* ancestors, believing all things written in the Law and the prophets" (emphases mine). Heresy is a means detractors and enemies use to delegitimate Christ-belief. Paul, in his reply, asserts that the label is misapplied. The Jesus Movement worships the Jewish God and believes in Jewish scripture. It is no heresy.

So what constitutes heresy in Acts? The label is used for competing groups that are explicitly identified as being Jewish. Acts 5:17 claims that adherents to "the heresy (αἵρεσις) of the Sadducees" are responsible for arresting Peter and John after they perform public miracles that lead to mass conversion. Acts 15:5 names Pharisees as heretics (αἱρέσεως) who object to Paul's preaching. Paul uses αἵρεσιν to speak of his former affiliation as a Pharisee as well, saying he lived "according to the most exact heresy (αἵρεσιν) of [his] religion" (26:5). Coupled with denials that αἵρεσις applies to the Jesus Movement, these uses demonstrate that heresy is an othering label as early as Acts. Luke uses the category to frame the Jesus Movement as not-heresy, that is, as the legitimate worship of the Jewish God. Simultaneously, he characterizes Jewish heresies as being arrayed against his protagonists. In the end, these rhetorical moves center the Jesus Movement, and Jesus, as a culmination of Jewish law and prophecy (28:23).

How does μαγεία fit into Acts' origins story for Christianity? Luke uses it when describing ritual experts or their expertise, quite like Matthew. Luke's protagonists are superior to their magician rivals, the latter of whom try to usurp apostolic authority or impede the gospel.[75] Consider Simon of Samaria, who is explicitly described as "doing magic" (μαγεύων, at 8:9) (8:6–11). The feats Simon performs are so extraordinary that he gathers a large following among the Samaritans (8:10). They even declare him "the power of God called 'great'" (8:10–11). But Simon's charisma and skill prove no match for leaders of the

---

[75] On Paul as "apostle": Acts 14:1–18, esp. 14:14.

Jesus Movement. When Philip arrives in Samaria and begins performing wonders, it is Simon who finds himself enchanted (8:12). Simon is even baptized alongside his former devotees (8:13). Things take a sharp turn when Peter and John arrive to confer the Holy Spirit upon the new converts (8:14). Simon sees the two laying hands and conferring the Spirit, and is so impressed that he offers to purchase this ability. He says to Peter, "Give to me also this authority (ἐξουσίαν) so that the one on whom I lay my hands might receive the Holy Spirit" (8:19). This request goes badly. Peter rebukes him, and Simon exits the scene after begging the apostle to pray for him (8:23–24). He never appears again in Acts, though Simon has quite the afterlife in later Christian texts. Acts 13:4–12 introduces another magician (μάγον, at 13:6) named Bar-Jesus. This man is a "Jewish false prophet" who likely serves as a court adviser to the Roman proconsul, Sergius Paulus (13:6). Bar-Jesus runs afoul of Paul. Having heard about the Jesus Movement, Sergius Paulus summons Paul and Barnabas to learn more (13:6–7). But Bar-Jesus intervenes and tries to turn the man away from Paul's teachings (13:8). Paul, like Peter, responds with biting invective, calling Bar-Jesus "son of the devil," "enemy of all righteousness," and "full of deceit and fraud" (13:10). Since he tried to obstruct the "paths of the Lord", this magician will be unable to see temporarily (13:10–11).[76] This pericope ends with Bar-Jesus being led away in disgrace after a blinding mist falls over his eyes (13:11). Like Simon, he never reappears.

These two magicians have unsettled fates, since we do not know if Simon's prayers were answered or what happened when Bar-Jesus regained his sight. Still, we can make some assertions. These two share clear resemblances to the magicians in Matthew 2:1–16. All of them have ritual expertise, either charismatic (Simon's wonderworking) or demonstrated by their proximity to imperial authorities. In Matthew 2:8 and Acts 13:6, magicians advise Herod and Sergius Paulus, respectively. This characterization aligns with broader stereotypes of magicians as part of a massive, undifferentiated class of ritual experts who were thought to offer a range of services.[77] Simon and Bar-Jesus cannot be favorably viewed, though. They do not submit to Christian leaders and instead try to usurp these leaders' authority or obstruct their mission. It is difficult to state, conclusively, why both of their stories are open-ended. Is there room for them to be redeemed? Some clues can be found elsewhere, specifically pericopae where Luke unceremoniously dispatches characters who subvert divine power or apostolic authority. Acts 5:1–11 shows Peter killing Ananias and Sapphira because they lied to God and further lied to and

---

[76] I cannot responsibly address ableism in early Christian texts. See instead the *status quaestiones* essay by Soon, 2021.
[77] Wendt, 2016, pp. 114–145.

tested the Holy Spirit (5:3–5, 9). In 12:20–23, Herod dresses in the finest royal raiment to publicly address a large crowd. When they declare that he speaks with the "voice of God," Herod is struck down for not properly glorifying God (12:23). Compared to other characters who transgress community norms, Simon and Bar-Jesus have relatively happy endings. Whatever their transgressions, they do not require a death sentence. Perhaps the magicians might be redeemed if they defer to the designated leaders of the Jesus Movement?

At the very least, magicians' fates are undetermined in Acts. We have surer footing when we consider the broader ramifications of these stories. Peter and Paul easily overpower Simon and Bar-Jesus, which is unsurprising since they are Luke's protagonists. Still, their being placed in apposition to two magicians invites comparison. In my view, the difference between magicians and apostles in Acts is about access to divine power. Peter and Paul receive the power of the Holy Spirit directly from Christ (Peter in 1:5, 8, and 2:1–4; Paul, by way of Ananias, in 9:17–19). The Spirit drives the apostles' mission (1:8). Rival experts like magicians cannot have the same access, and so they are excluded from the Jesus Movement when they attempt to usurp the Holy Spirit's power or to thwart the apostles' Spirit-driven ministry. Similar to αἵρεσις, μαγεία is co-constitutive with formative Christianity. Magic marks outsiders, but it also provides a foil against which Luke defines apostolic authority. Peter and Paul are superior ritual experts, and they are superior precisely because they carry out their duties for Christ. Simon and Bar-Jesus are made into examples; they show what happens to would-be usurpers or obstructors. Acts initiates one of the preeminent indices that later writers will use to distinguish Christian orthodoxy – apostolic succession, which depends on such negotiations of apostolic authority. The Jesus Movement, like other groups, has a leadership hierarchy. And Luke cautions real or imagined rivals to Jesus' apostles: Expertise is no guarantor of authority.

Coda: Magic, Heresy, and Formative Christianity

If this survey of αἵρεσις and μαγεία in first-century Christian texts forms the conceptual baseline for later writings, what might we conclude at this juncture? First, I think we must own that magic and heresy do not clearly intersect, with the possible exception of φαρμακεία in Gal. 5:20. The two categories do, however, help authors circumscribe the contours of Christ-belief in opposition to either magic or heresy. On its surface, αἵρεσις denotes schisms, but when we look at its function in conjunction with this seemingly neutral definition, heresy's potential for discursive disciplining comes to the fore. It is not a neutral category describing distinct religious or epistemic systems. Rather, it works to elevate earliest Christianity over and above these competing systems.

In canonical epistles, heretics foment schisms because they do not properly adhere to authors' salvific teachings. When used as a verb, heresy presents a binary choice between salvation and condemnation. In Acts, αἵρεσις refers to other Jewish groups, but never to the Jesus Movement. Ultimately, this decenters Judaism as the legitimate worship of the Jewish God and centers Christ-belief instead. As Le Boulluec argues, these early uses of heresy are not solely about orthopraxy. Canonical texts all intimate that adherence to or deviance from community norms are precipitated by teachings – those belonging to Paul's much-maligned enemies in Galatia, for example, or to Sadducees and Pharisees. These "others" to formative Christianity throw into sharp relief the boundaries of the in-group that the canonical texts construct. Here, formative Christianity is paradoxically Jewish and not: It appropriates Jewish tradition and scripture while differentiating Christ-belief from Jewish heresies.

For these authors, μαγεία is most commonly the purview of ritual experts – of magicians. Emphasis on expertise is further reflected in the relationships authors create between magicians and Christian heroes: Jesus, Peter, and Paul. Magic does not denote a sphere of belief and/or praxis that is ever in tension with Christ-belief in earliest texts. Matthew's Gospel even views magical expertise favorably, though Luke's assessment is admittedly more complicated. Magicians in Acts are excoriated by their apostolic counterparts, but unlike other characters who transgress group norms, magicians are allowed to live. Magic is used for various ends here: to substantiate Jesus' identity, to dazzle crowds, or as one tool among many, likely as part of a court adviser's repertoire. Magicians, like heresies, help define the Christian other. For an audience familiar with stereotypes of magic and magic-users, these texts argue that Christian leaders are superior, either inherently (Matthew's Jesus) or because they have access to the Holy Spirit (Peter and Paul in Acts). Later Christian writers used these negotiations to develop the notion of apostolic succession – a defining criterion for proto-orthodoxy.[78]

In the introduction, I argued that disciplinary discourses engender epistemicide, since they sharpen dynamic and unwieldy categories into increasingly narrow rhetorical weapons. In formative Christian texts, heresy makes and marks difference between Christ-belief and Judaism(s). Sadducees, Pharisees, and those preaching adherence to Mosaic Law foment heresies – a label rarely used to describe authors' own teachings. As a verb too, αἱρέω does disciplinary work. Moses and the Jewish God choose the saving gospel of Christ. The category of magic seems less rigid in comparison. Certainly, magicians lurk within canonical texts, but they are rare. When they appear,

---

[78] Irenaeus, *Adv. Haer.* 3.1.1; Tertullian, *Praescr.* 22.9–11.

they appear alongside leaders (or founders) of the Jesus Movement. First-century writers applaud magicians who recognize their betters and punish those who wish to usurp apostolic authority or thwart the gospel. Of special note is Acts' ambiguous attitude, demonstrated by the unsettled fates of Simon and Bar-Jesus. But whatever the case in Acts, any avenue for magicians' redemption is closed in the second-century CE. Heresiology demands tidy taxonomies where competing religious and epistemic systems are classed as either orthodoxy or heresy. Almost by default, magicians become heresiarchs – malicious and depraved ritual experts who revel in demon-olatry and lead others astray.

The Long Shadow of Emergent Heresiology: The Second Century

The second-century CE is commonly viewed as the era of emergent heresiology, a period that witnesses Christian authors making and marking difference against specific theological or doctrinal positions and/or groups deemed heretical. Writers of this period use αἵρεσις/*haeresis* to promote group cohesion like their predecessors. But the taxon expands in critical ways. Early exemplars forge conceptual links between heretical schismatics and sin. By the mid second century, heresy becomes something like an epistemology – a mode of thinking, of meaning-making, that will cast long shadows over subsequent Christian literature. Second-century heresiological thinking becomes even sharper when it leverages reigning notions of μαγεία/*magia*. Toward the end of this period, magic becomes a shorthand for religious deviance. When magic meets heresy, the result is doubly reinforcing: Heretics use magic, and using magic makes one a heretic by default. This discursive intersection is most visible in "magician-heresiarch" figures like those we meet in Irenaeus of Lyons, whose *Against Heresies* forms the case study for this section. Irenaeus uses ritual experts as conceptual foils his own apostolic and decidedly not magical orthodoxy. So while this era does not yet offer a totalizing conflation of magic-heresy like we find in Augustine and his late ancient contemporaries, these texts reflect how rapidly the conceptual landscape was shifting, and, in addition, how quickly reductive binaries were imposed upon a vast matrix of religious and epistemic systems.

Before we consider any Christian texts, it is important to summarize two developments that characterize this period: (1) the coalescing of a "strong notion" of magic; and (2) the advent of heresiology. By "strong notion," I mean the category of magic gets disciplined in order to enforce the boundaries of proper religion. While this disciplining had been going on for centuries, the second century results in a predominating, negative view of magic that was imported into the Roman imaginary.[79] Such a strong notion of magic proliferates in the literary record, including Jewish and Christian writings that frame magic as a demonolatrous engine for heresy-making.[80] In legal writings, magic gets criminalized as a form of religious transgression with increasing regularity until associations between magic and criminal religious deviance are formalized around the early third-century CE.[81] A second and equally important trend involves the development of heresiology, a genre of writing expressly aimed at ordering competing religious and epistemic systems to make and mark doctrinal error and theological difference.[82] Of course, heresiological thinking – making and marking difference in a more general fashion – precedes heresiology proper.[83] But once heresiologists like Irenaeus combine contemporaneous views of magic and heresy, the two discourses become forever linked. Magic gets tied to heresy in ways that will escape the confines of this literary genre and that will inflect most subsequent Christian literature. Late ancient totalizing conflations of magic-heresy could not have happened without the discursive disciplining of the second-century CE.

Heresy to Heresiology

Christian writings in this period see a marked shift between uses of αἵρεσις/ *haeresis* before the emergence of heresiology versus after. But while heresiology engenders new modes of making and marking difference, it does not emerge in a conceptual vacuum.[84] Writers in the first half of this century incorporated ideas about sin, evil, and the demonic in their heresiological projects, ultimately making heresy sinful by default.

I want to begin with two texts that could belong to the late first or early second century CE: 2 Peter and the *Shepherd of Hermas*.[85] These texts anticipate the emergence of heresiology as epistemology – a discussion that makes more sense in this section than in the preceding one. 2 Peter classes heresy as bad knowledge while *Hermas* views it as flatly demonic. Both use heresy to authorize preferred ways of transmitting knowledge. 2 Peter relies on its (false) claim to Petrine authorship in order to warn against "false teachers" who introduce "destructive heresies" (αἱρέσεις ἀπωλείας, at 2:1)

---

[79] Gordon, 1999, pp. 164–165; cf., Dickie, 2008, p. 127; Stratton, 2007, pp. 105–106.
[80] See Stratton's masterful distillation of the literary stereotype: 2007, pp. 71–106; in Christian literature especially: pp. 107–141. Stratton also summarizes the treatment of Jewish evidence in Garrett, 1989, pp. 37–78.
[81] Rives, 2003, pp. 327–328. [82] Smith, 2014, pp. 11–21.
[83] Royalty, 2015, esp. pp. 35–41; Simon, 1979, p. 109. [84] Royalty, 2015, p. 68.
[85] 2 Peter and *Hermas* are difficult to date. 2 Peter is dated between the end of the first and beginning of the second-century CE: Coogan et al., 2001, p. 401 (NT). I mention its resemblance to Pauline discourses of heresy in From Christ-Beliefs to Christianity: The First Century; here I consider its fuller role in heresiological thinking before the advent of heresy. For *Hermas*, I follow Ehrman's dating between 110 and 140 CE (LCL 25: Ehrman, 2003b, p. 169).

and "fabricated teachings" (πλαστοῖς λόγοις, at 2:3). These teachers do not stop at creating schisms; they engage in all manner of sin, from blasphemy (2:2–3), to sexual immorality, to greed (2:4–16). 2 Peter dehumanizes heretics and their teachings, the latter of which are steeped in "animalistic irrationality" (ἄλογα ζῷα, 2:12). For its part, *Hermas* makes heresy flatly demonic. The text purportedly relates visions and angelic pronouncements directly handed down to the author.[86] One proclamation appears in 100.1–3. Here, individuals who foment schisms are depicted as doing so out of anger and malice. This, in turn, prompts God to reject them. The angel then continues: "to all who hold this heresy (αἵρεσιν, referring to the schisms in 100.1–3), let it go and repent, and the Lord will heal your former sins, if you cleanse yourselves of this demon" (100.5).[87] When read together, these two authors articulate early ideas that will receive much fuller elaboration in heresiology: Heresy is bad or corrupted knowledge (2 Peter 2:3) that is inherently demonic (*Hermas* 100.5). It has disreputable origins in human anger and malice (*Hermas* 100.1–3), or carnality and irrationality (2 Peter 2:12). These two texts also share a self-authorizing strategy. 2 Peter appeals to its authorial claim (1:16–18), whereas *Hermas* appeals to the angelic source of its revelatory knowledge (100.5). Authors' emphasis on epistemic authority – on who knows enough to accurately identify heresy – becomes an especially powerful rhetorical tool in the hands of heresiologists.

Similar preoccupations with epistemic authority appear in the writings of Ignatius of Antioch (d. ca. 98–117 CE).[88] Ignatius pens several letters on his way to his own execution. Throughout, he leverages αἵρεσις to legitimate bishops as the sole locus of truth.[89] Scholars have rigorously identified many of the individual views Ignatius polemicizes against, from docetic Christologies to "Judaizing".[90] Analyzing how he uses αἵρεσις does not require such granularity, though, precisely because Ignatius deploys the label against any teachings that do not come from a bishop. In *Eph.* 6.2, he praises the Ephesians because they "live in accordance with truth and no heresy (αἵρεσις) has taken hold among [them]."[91] The harmony within their community parallels Christ's harmonious existence with the church and with God (5.1–2). Because their bishop's mind is ever-aligned with Christ's (3.3), the Ephesians know their leader always speaks the truth (6.2). Obeying the bishop is tantamount to obeying the Lord (6.1). Ignatius explicitly says heresy

---

[86] Ehrman, 2003b, pp. 162–165.   [87] Greek from LCL 25, p. 444.
[88] Dating in LCL 24: Ehrman, 2003a, p. 203.
[89] Ehrman, 2003a, p. 203. On Ignatius' heresiological contribution: Royalty, 2015, p. 137.
[90] Review of this scholarship in Lookadoo, 2023, pp. 12–15; cf., Ehrman, 2003a, pp. 206–209.
[91] Greek from LCL 24, p. 224.

is an external imposition on truth. In *Trall.* 6.2, he claims false teachers feed unsuspecting believers a "foreign plant, which is heresy" (αἵρεσις).[92] This potion (φάρμακον, at *Trall.* 6.2) is an impure adulteration of the truth (*Trall.* 6.1–7.2). To guard against heretics' corrupting poisons, one should heed the bishop (*Trall.* 7.1). Ignatius clearly appropriates and reconfigures earlier applications of αἵρεσις. Like canonical epistles, he credits false teachers with fomenting disharmonious heresies. He locates true knowledge as belonging exclusively to an authorized knower – the bishop. But Ignatius also expands the scope of heresy, which takes on a more generalizing force in his oeuvre since it applies to all unauthorized teachings. In this way, Ignatius is able to center a tightly circumscribed proto-orthodoxy over and against several heresies. These letters also elevate an emerging ecclesiastical hierarchy, and Ignatius' use of αἵρεσις plays a key role in legitimating the episcopacy.

The advent of heresiology amplifies such views of heresy as schism, false teaching, sin, and bad or corrupted knowledge. The terms αἵρεσις/*haeresis* acquire an intensely pejorative force here.[93] We have seen pejorative uses of αἵρεσις in earlier texts, though, so how does its use differ in heresiology? For one, the second-century CE historical context demands sharper modes of making and marking difference. Christianity is becoming visible as a distinct tradition; it is being "invented" through successive cycles of self-fashioning.[94] But it is not standardized. Diverse Christianities proliferate, prompting writers of this period to insulate their own orthodoxies against competing religious and epistemic traditions, including other Christianities. For instance, Justin Martyr (d. ca. 165 CE) reframes heresy to designate "'sects' who falsely arrogate to themselves the name of 'Christian' and whose opinions ... are contrary to the precepts of Christ."[95] He uses the category to mark other Christians as "not Christian," in sum. This is only possible because Justin assumes a coherent Christianity, an orthodoxy, from which heresies deviate.

I think heresiology makes a second innovation, too. It makes heresy into an epistemic system of sorts, by which I mean a way of knowing and assessing religious and epistemic rivals. Certainly, earlier Christian writers make similar gestures. So, in Gal. 5:13–2, when Paul places αἱρέσεις alongside other "works of the flesh," he offers a way of assessing schism and schism-fomenting teachers. He prescribes a means to negotiate conflicting teachings. Heresiologies also have prescriptive inertia, but they craft a much broader framework for heresy. In part, we might attribute this conceptual expansion to Christianity's invention, but genre

---

[92] LCL 24, p. 262.   [93] Le Boulluec, 2022, p. 30.
[94] Eshleman, 2012, esp. pp. 149–176, covers the second and third centuries.
[95] Le Boulluec, 2022, p. 30.

conventions also play a role. Heresiologies often feature genealogies of supposed heretics that detail and refute their beliefs and practices.[96] Even in the absence of genealogies, these texts describe the religious and epistemic systems of their avowed opponents. The very project of heresiology positions the heresiologist as a "knower."[97] But someone like Irenaeus of Lyons (d. ca. 200–203 CE) knows about more than his immediate opponents and their teachings. His *Against Heresies* presupposes an essential notion of heresy – of what makes heresy heretical. This is why Irenaeus can so confidently assess a great many religious and epistemic rivals, past and present. He then transmits this knowledge to his audience, teaching them how to assess the selfsame rivals.

Heresiology's epistemic project, and the accompanying shift in αἵρεσις, is especially visible in the works of Justin Martyr (d. ca. 165 CE), an architect of the genre and quite possibly the author of the first known heresiological work.[98] This work, the *Syntagma*, is now lost, but we can see how the category of heresy becomes an epistemology in surviving works.[99] Justin's *Apologies* use rhetorical strategies common to heresiology. In *Apol.* 1.26.1–8, he discusses the teachings of Simon, Menander, and Marcion, all of which he calls heresies (αἱρέσεων, at 1.26.8). Heresies are derivative and antecedent to truth. After Christ ascended, Justin claims, demons instigated the elevation of certain men who claimed to be gods (1.26.1).[100] One of these men, Simon, convinced denizens of Rome that he was divine by using demonic assistance to perform magical acts (ποιήσας μαγικὰς, at 1.26.2). But Simon's heresy-making did not end there. His disciple, Menander, also spread falsehoods through the same magical skill (μαγικῆς τέχνης, at 26.5).[101] Finally, Justin mentions Marcion, the preeminent heretic in early Christian literature, though surprisingly, Justin does not explicitly accuse Marcion of using magic (1.26.5). Simon, Menander, and Marcion spread falsehoods among all nations (1.26.2–5). But despite their demonolatry and error, "those who hasten to [these men] are called 'Christians' (26.6)."

A similar dilemma must have plagued many of Justin's contemporaries. What to do with individuals or groups who self-identify or are recognized as Christians, but who trade in falsehoods? I think an expansive notion of heresy helps Justin resolve this problem. To assess "non-Christian" Christians, he relies on knowledge of mythic history – which, in turn, positions him as knower of this very history. In *Apol.* 2.5.2, Justin reconstructs a genealogy of truth, or

---

[96] Discussions in: Buell, 1999, pp. 79–93; Cameron, 2003, pp. 476–477; Flower, 2010, esp. pp. 73–77.
[97] Flower, 2010, pp. 77–78, details this trend in Epiphanius.
[98] Discussion in Royalty, 2015, pp. 16–20. Smith discusses and disputes Justin's authorship of the *Syntagma*: 2014, pp. 49–86.
[99] Dating: Smith, 2014, p. 5, n. 9.   [100] Greek from Migne PG 6.369.48.
[101] PG 6.368.35, PG 6.368.41.

true knowledge, originating in the primeval past.[102] Long ago, long before Christ's incarnation even, fallen angels-turned-demons subjugated humanity through magical writings (μαγικῶν γραφῶν), fear of punishment, and paganisms (2.5.2).[103] True Christians are not subject to these things, however. In contrast to heresies rooted in demonic knowledges, true Christians adhere to a universal and eternal truth preceding all rival religious and epistemic systems (*Apol.* 1.16.14).[104] In fact, Justin refuses to call adherents to heresies "Christians," instead referring to them "by the name of the progenitor of [their] false doctrine" (*Dial.* 35.4). This narrows Justin's (proto-)orthodoxy over and against all other systems, the latter of which have demonic origins. Justin's rhetorical moves constitute an epistemology, a way of knowing and assessing religious and epistemic rivals to true Christianity. Only those who subscribe to the same eternal and transcendent truth as Justin can rightly be called "Christian."[105]

Justin makes μαγεία the tool of demonolatrous heretics who delight in prompting apostasy. In his genealogy of true and demonic knowledges, magic could never offer truth. It can only be a tool for promoting heresy. Magic and heresy meet in earlier texts, but not quite like in Justin or in heresiologies.

Toward a "Strong Notion" of Magic

Justin and his contemporaries use the category μαγεία/*magia* in seemingly-diffuse ways, but it eventually gets sharpened into a rhetorical weapon for policing what we moderns might call religious deviance. In the first half of this century, magic gets linked with sin and condemnation. After the emergence of heresiology, it becomes a fairly commonplace way of othering competing religious and epistemic systems.

Early second-century texts like the *Didache* and the *Epistle of Barnabas* class μαγεία as an irredeemable sin that necessarily leads to condemnation.[106] The *Didache* and *Barnabas* gain a lot of rhetorical leverage from what scholars call the "doctrine of the two ways."[107] This doctrine, much like the verb αἱρέω in canonical texts, imposes a binary between two eschatological outcomes: The righteous "way of life" leads to salvation, but if one should travel along the

---

[102] On genealogies in Justin: Le Boulluec, 2022, pp. 80–87. Doxographies in Justin: Le Boulluec, 2022, pp. 33–42. Heresiological doxographies in general: Smith, 2014, pp. 1–48.

[103] Greco-Roman philosophy is a notable exception to this demonization: Le Boulluec, 2022, pp. 46–47; cf. *Dial.* 2.1–2. On Justin's appropriation of the Enochic Tradition: Reed, 2004; cf., Stratton, 2007, pp. 120–121.

[104] Le Boulluec, 2022, p. 30; Royalty, 2015, pp. 7–8.   [105] Le Boulluec, 2022, pp. 55–57.

[106] Ehrman gives a date of 100–110 CE for the Didache: 2003a, p. 411. For *Barnabas*, ca. 130 CE: 2003b, p. 7.

[107] Ehrman, 2003a, pp. 406–407.

accursed "way of death," they will be condemned. Both texts list magic among the many vices that mark this path to death. In the *Didache*, magic (μαγεῖαι) and potions (φαρμακίαι) are viewed akin to a bevy of sins, including but not limited to adultery, idolatry, theft, and sexual immorality (5.1).[108] *Barnabas* has a nearly identical list, likely on account of shared sources.[109] Here too μαγεία and φαρμακεία appear in a catalog of soul-destroying sins (20.1).[110] Magic is more than a sin, though. Both texts impugn those who use it, elaborating on the evilness of travelers who walk the path of death. These individuals, including magic-users, persecute the good, hate truth, and love lies (*Didache* 5.2; *Barnabas* 20.2). They corrupt what God has made (*Didache* 5.2; *Barnabas* 20.2) and behave abominably toward poor and vulnerable people (*Didache* 5.2; *Barnabas* 20.2). Texts like the *Didache* and *Barnabas* seem far more assured of magicians' irredeemability than canonical predecessors. We should note, too, the inclusion of μαγεία alongside φαρμακεία, suggesting that these authors wish to criticize magic as such, alongside individual practices like enchantment.

Elsewhere in second-century Christian literature, magic is used to mark religious and epistemic others to proto-orthodoxy. Ignatius, for one, makes an especially telling equivalence between Judaism and magic. He claims all μαγεία and bondage to evil are part of an "ancient realm" which obtained through ignorance, but which was destroyed via the incarnation of Christ (*Eph.* 19.3).[111] In other letters, we get clues about the nature of this ancient realm. *Phil.* 8.2 refers to Jewish scriptures as "ancient writings" (8.2). *Magnesians* warns its audience not to be deceived by "heterodoxies (ἑτεροδοξίαις) or ancient myths" – alluding again to Judaism, which is excluded from God's grace (8.2).[112] *Magn.* 9.2 calls Sabbath observance the "ancient way." The ancient magical realm in *Eph.* 19.3 is Judaism. By describing it as magical, Ignatius advances a supersessionist program of delegitimizing Judaism by associating it with a category that is increasingly used to mark religious deviance during this period. In his letters, both magic and Judaism become a foil for his new orthodoxy, which is free of ignorance, primitivism, and evil. It is worth noting that magic long retains its use as a foil for correct piety and reason, and even for modernity, especially in Western European intellectual history.[113]

Magic is used to other religious or epistemic rivals in apocryphal texts, too. One early example can be found in the *Acts of John* (*Acts John*). Generally speaking, these acts are highly fictionalized accounts of the apostles' missionary travels. *Acts John*, for its part, makes Roman paganism magical.[114] Consider a particularly riotous story that occurs at the famous temple of Artemis in

---

[108] LCL 24, p. 426.   [109] Ehrman, 2003b, p. 7.   [110] LCL 25, p. 80.   [111] LCL 24, p. 238.
[112] LCL 24, p. 248.   [113] See the monograph-length study by Styers, 2008.
[114] On dating: Elliott, 1993, p. 306.

Ephesus. When John arrives before a crowd of Artemis-worshippers who wish to enter the temple, he issues a far-fetched ultimatum – either they will convert or he will die by Artemis' hand (40.3). John then starts to pray, with his prayer resulting in rather a lot of destruction: The temple's altar crumbles, its votives topple, idols break, and Artemis' priest is crushed when half the building collapses (42.1). John attributes this destruction to his God. He asks his audience why, if she were so powerful, does Artemis not stop him from destroying the temple (43.5). "Where are her festivals?" he taunts, "Where are her wreaths? Where is all the magic (μαγεία) and enchantment (φαρμακεία), her sister?" (43.5). *Acts John* claims that paganism, represented by the worship of Artemis, necessarily involves magic and enchantment. In contrast, the "wonders" (θαυμάσια, at 42.2) John performs are so impressive that Ephesian pagans immediately convert, despite seeing their place of worship destroyed (40.3). In fact, they destroy the rest of the temple themselves (44.1). It is difficult to imagine the sort of worshipper who would readily convert after seeing their place of worship destroyed by another god. Perhaps the point of this story in *Acts John* lies in showcasing the superiority of miracle over magic. I think so, at least in part. But it also does something more subtle. *Acts John* layers a binary between Christianity and paganism atop the "magic versus miracle" contest. Here, magic's other is not simply miracle; it is *Christianity* – indicated by mass conversion.

Texts from this period leverage μαγεία to mark sinfulness or to delegitimate rival religious and epistemic systems. The *Didache* and *Barnabas* vilify those who might use magic as being inherently sinful and malicious. Magic-users are evil by default, and there is no room to rehabilitate them. Other texts like Ignatius' letters and *Acts John* suggest that religious or epistemic rivals to Christianity, or at least facets of these systems, are magical. These uses of magic seem scattershot at first glance, but all of these writers are picking up on a "strong notion" of magic that coalesces in this period. Magic can refer to all manner of phenomena, but here we see it being used to indicate religious deviance. We should not be surprised to see the accusation of magic levied at Jews and pagans; they are religious others to the Christianity being invented in the second century.

Case Study: Magician-Heresiarchs in Irenaeus of Lyons

Discourses of magic and heresy meet in the second-century CE. In Christian texts, the process of making magic co-equal to heresy gains a great deal of rhetorical currency from the magician-heresiarch figures we meet in heresiologies. These transgressive ritual experts become convenient foils for our authors' orthodoxies. I would argue that we still do not have a totalizing magic-heresy conflation in this era, but we certainly have authors lengthening the conceptual distance between their orthodoxies and magic. Irenaeus of Lyons (d. ca. 200–203 CE) exemplifies this trend by intensifying anti-magic polemic against magician-heresiarchs.

Completed around 180 CE, Irenaeus' five-volume *Against Heresies* was wildly influential among later Christian writers.[115] In *Haer.* 1.23.2, our author claims Simon of Samaria is the progenitor of all heresies (*ex quo universae haereses substiterunt*).[116] Such an accusation represents an obvious departure from Acts 8, so Irenaeus must fill in some details. He says that Simon did indeed convert to Christianity, but was not content to remain adherent and instead devoted himself to all magical arts (*universam magicam*, at 1.23.1). Simon wished to be greater than the apostles and win over multitudes of followers (1.23.1). The magician-heresiarch was very successful at this, ultimately being honored as a god himself (1.23.1). His followers, self-styled "Simonians," disseminated his teachings, which Irenaeus describes as "falsely-called 'knowledge'" (*falsi nominis scientia*, at 1.23.4).[117] Among this false knowledge, we find practices associated with magic like exorcisms (*exorcismis*), incantations (*incantantiabus*), love spells (*amatoria*), charms (*agogima*), and the use of demonic helpers called *parhedroi* (*paredri*) (1.23.4).

When delegitimizing heresies derivative of Simonism, Irenaeus imparts to each at least one shared characteristic with the version of Simonism he posits in 1.23.1–4.[118] Since all heresies originate with Simon, they are genetically linked and therefore implicated in magic (1.30.15).[119] Irenaeus goes beyond linking all heresies to magic. He also uses contemporary stereotypes of magic and magicians to reinforce the illegitimacy of heresy. The accrual of anti-magic tropes reaches a height in the figure of Marcus, a magician-heresiarch clearly patterned after Simon. Like his heretical forefather, Marcus is proficient in magical trickery (μαγικῆς ὑπάρχων κυβείας ἐμπειρότατος/*magicae imposturae pertissimus*, at 1.13.1).[120] He gains followers by combining the facetious teachings of Anaxilaus and magicians (μάγων/*magi*, at 1.13.1). Irenaeus also numbers Marcus' many misdeeds, accusing him of fabricating his own mockery of the Eucharist (1.13.2); idol-making (1.14.3); employing a *parhedros* (πάρεδρον/*paredrum*, at 1.13.3) to prophesy and to grant this ability to others (and especially to women); holding debauched feasts (1.13.4); and concocting

---

[115] Le Boulluec, 2022, p. 110. Only selections of the Greek survive, though the entirety is preserved in a later Latin translation. I gloss both Greek and Latin where available.
[116] Latin and Greek from BSS, 3, pp. 246–247.   [117] BSS 3, p. 250.   [118] Haar, 2003, p. 19.
[119] Buell, 1999, pp. 79–93; Cameron, 2003, pp. 476–477; Flower, 2010, p. 74.
[120] BSS 3, pp. 170–171.

potions and love spells (φίλτρα καὶ ἀγώγιμα/*amatoria et adlectantia*, at 1.13.5) for the purposes of sexual assault (1.13.5–7).[121] To cap it all, Marcus blasphemes, insisting he has knowledge not even other gods have (1.14.1).

It is difficult to imagine a more stereotypical magician than Marcus, a figure who embodies so many contemporary ideas about magicians. Magicians were indeed thought to use helper demons like *parhedroi* who completed various tasks for them.[122] They were accused of being sexually transgressive or immoral, exemplified by their purported proficiency with love spells.[123] They enjoyed the sort of debauchery that proliferated at Marcus' feasts. Even Irenaeus' mention of Anaxilaus is anti-magic polemic.[124] By leveraging these popular stereotypes, Irenaeus makes magicians into the quintessential and original heretics. Concomitantly, he implies that magic is implicated in heresy-making. This combination of magic and heresy offers a potent, dually reinforcing expedient against opponents. Not only do these magician-heresiarchs spread falsehoods, they do so through demonic magic. Once such conceptual connections are forged, they become increasingly stabilized. Magicians are by default heretics, and magic is well on its way to being heresy, not just making it.

Coda: The Second Century's Long Shadows

In many ways, the second-century CE is the most transformative period in the genealogy of magic and heresy I trace throughout this Element. Here is where αἵρεσις/*haeresis* and μαγεία/*magia* acquire their sharpest contours, not because our authors place magic in apposition to miracle, but because they make magic the obverse of Christianity. Perhaps it is most accurate to say magic is a kind of bad or corrupted knowledge that drives heresies. Those who dabble in it must be heretics, since it relies on demonic assistance and is inherently evil. And heretics, especially the popular ones, use magic to spread their lies. In sum, magic becomes the preeminent tool for heresy-making.

We lose this emphasis on ritual expertise and knowledge – this nuance – in later texts. Christians writing in the third and fourth centuries tend to disparage magic in the abstract, ultimately forging what Maijastina Kahlos calls a "magicless" Christianity.[125]

---

[121] BSS 3: πάρεδρος/*paredrum*, p. 173; φίλτρα καὶ ἀγώγιμα/*amatoria et adlectantia*, p. 177.
[122] Graf, 1997, pp. 107–116.
[123] Graf, 1997, pp. 176–190. The clearly gendered nature of this discourse is beyond the scope of this project. Instead, consult Stratton, 2007, pp. 71–105.
[124] Anaxilaus is elsewhere associated with magic: Le Boulluec, 2022, p. 113 n. 13–14; cf., Jerome, *Chron.* 163.26–164.2; Pliny, *HN*, 35.15. On broader associations between magic and philosophy: Wendt, 2016, pp. 114–145.
[125] Kahlos, 2020, p. 128.

The second century's rigid discursive disciplining occurs on two fronts corresponding to wider literary and cultural developments. With respect to heresy, this period sees the label honed into a means for making and marking demonolatrous and erroneous teachings proffered by false teachers. As Christians learned to define themselves over and against religious and epistemic others, heresy became a means for circumscribing true Christianity, or orthodoxy. At the same time, magic acquires the force of "religious deviance" in broader discourses. Once heresiologists claim that demonolatrous magic is responsible for the spread of erroneous heresies, there is no turning back.

Christian literature of this period helps to answer one of the questions that prompted this Element: How does magic, a label applied to ritual practices, become the illicit obverse of an entire religious or epistemic system? To put it another way: Would not miracle be the natural conceptual other for magic? Why does magic acquire enough conceptual heft to stand in tension with Christianity? Paradoxically, this expansion is a site of epistemicide. Writers who frame magic as a tool for heresy-making unmoor it from the practices that comprised a stereotype of magic in the ancient Roman imagination. Instead of assessing a given practice in context, now the audience receives a prescription for assessing magic as such. Likewise, the simultaneous disciplining of heresy means that Christian leaders like Marcus and Simon cannot be viewed as real Christians. Like Paul, heresiologists leave no room for other gospels. So, while I do not think we have the totalizing overlap between magic and heresy that characterizes late antiquity yet, this period clearly anticipates it.

The "magic versus orthodoxy" binary erected here casts long shadows over late ancient Christianity and far beyond. Early associations among magic, demonism, sin, and heresy discipline both categories and make them powerful rhetorical tools against real or perceived enemies. And writers we encounter in this section help invent "Christianity" by negotiating their own orthodoxies against heretical others, and then, by reinscribing orthodoxy through iterative writing practices.[126] With the development of heresiology, Christian authors start anchoring discourses of magic and of heresy in magician-heresiarch figures like Simon and Marcus. Such figures tie together broader ideas related to heresy, theological deviance or error, and demonolatrous magic. This sort of discursive disciplining is especially clear in the literary afterlife of Simon of Samaria, who undergoes a dramatic recharacterization from bumbling would-be usurper in Acts to the willful and malicious enemy of God in Irenaeus.

If Simon's postcanonical character development is reflective of discursive disciplining, then we must remember that the conceptual associations he helps

---

[126] Eshleman, 2012, p. 1.

craft – between magic and heresy, on the one hand, and between orthodoxy and truth, on the other – are not stable. They must be maintained through writing and rewriting. Subsequent discursive disciplining strengthens these associations, such that, by Augustine's day, we no longer need a magician-heresiarch to anchor these divergent genealogies. In late antiquity, invoking either magic or heresy is sufficient to simultaneously invoke the other.

Between Ascendant Orthodoxy and Empire: The Third Century

The close association between αἵρεσις/*haeresis* and μαγεία/*magia* forged in second-century Christian literature casts long shadows, but neither category becomes static. On the contrary, heresy and magic still accrue new meanings, both when used independently and when deployed together. The third-century CE witnessed complex sociopolitical transformations within the Roman Empire including, but not limited to, the decline of the emperor's power, demographic shifts, and border tensions.[127] Christian discourses undergo significant reorientations as well.[128] Specifically, an increased visibility of various Christianities within the larger matrix of Roman religious and epistemic systems prompts internal and external differentiation. In terms of "internal" discourses, we see αἵρεσις/*haeresis* used to elevate favored religious authorities and emerging church hierarchies. But Christianity's ascendancy is a double-edged sword. Authors find themselves on the defensive against accusations of μαγεία/*magia*. Naturally, such accusations are not new to this period, but they take on greater urgency under the threat of looming persecution. We also see a continued and increasing use of magic to police proper religion. By 300 CE, *magia* is criminalized as a kind of religious transgression in Roman law.[129] And while we cannot assume Christians on the ground were aware of all these changes, or of any, literary evidence from this century clearly betrays anxieties about Christian miracles being viewed as magic. The authors discussed next must navigate between the legacy and appeal of Christianity's miracle tradition and the concurrent intensification of anti-magic views.[130] In response, Christian authors reorient extant notions of magic and heresy, leveraging the two categories toward resolving pressing problems that occur between ascendancy and empire, between authors' religious and epistemic inheritances and how Christianity coalesces in the Roman imaginary. Our case study, the *Refutation of All Heresies*, is reflective

---

[127] The reason for and precise nature of said "crises" are disputed. Selected studies include: Garnsey and Humphress, 2001; Loriot and Nony, 1997; Ziolkowski, 2011. For the religious context in particular: Baker-Brian and Lössl, 2018.
[128] Clarke, 2008, esp. pp. 625–628.   [129] Rives, 2003, pp. 333–334.
[130] On the appeal of Christian wonderworking: MacMullen, 1984, esp. pp. 25–42.

of discursive stability and change. Like second-century heresiologies, it combines the force of αἵρεσις with the disciplining role of μαγεία to make magic the purview of deceitful heretics teaching plagiarized falsehoods. But this text also innovates by making magic and heresy more expansive, and consequently, more available to delegitimate a wide array of religious and epistemic rivals at once.

Heresy and Empire

North African Christianity is a site of robust literary production in the third-century CE. The writings of Tertullian (d. after 220 CE) and Cyprian (d. 258 CE) offer us one widow onto developing Christian orthodoxy, its emergent authority structures and hierarchies, and how *haeresis* gets implicated in negotiations of religious authority. The real or perceived threat of persecution sends these two Carthaginian bishops scrambling to elevate their preferred authorities by marking other Christian leaders as heretics.[131] Tertullian uses heresy to malign the charismatic authority of martyrs while preserving the authority of the bishop of Rome. Cyprian is also interested in protecting ecclesiastical office, but he wields *haeresis* in a more generalizing fashion to re-authorize himself and the episcopacy as arbiters of orthodoxy. To be clear: Scholars are divided on the precise degree to which ecclesiastical hierarchies had been developed by this period.[132] The following discussion is not designed to resolve the matter but instead exposes discursive processes through which specific offices retained authority, no matter when these offices were first introduced. We will see why and how a newly disciplined category of heresy makes for so effective a rhetorical weapon, in other words.

Tertullian's (d. after 220 CE) extraordinary literary output makes him the preeminent figure of Latin Christianity.[133] His oeuvre includes heresiologies proper, but here I want to show how the notions of heresy forged in earlier Christian texts – including heresiologies – become agile rhetorical tools that respond to the contemporaneous issue of persecution. So, I want to consider Tertullian's defense of trinitarian theology, *Against Praxeas* (*Adv. Prax.*). This is one of his later writings, meaning we have surer footing for its inclusion among third-century texts.[134] *Adv. Prax.* uses *haeresis* to delegitimize martyrological authority while simultaneously elevating bureaucratic authorities. Especially fascinating is Tertullian's renegotiation of orthodoxy. He uses bureaucratic authority, in turn, to legitimate the New Prophecy, a Christian movement whose orthodoxy was in question – by Tertullian's own admission, no less.

---

[131] For a thoroughgoing treatment of historical realities and discursive constructions: Moss, 2012. For a concise digest: Clarke, 2008, pp. 616–625.
[132] Discussion in Slootjes, 2011, pp. 100–105.   [133] Dunn, 2004b, pp. 1–7.
[134] Dunn, 2004b, p. 5.

We know that contact and conflict with empire sometimes resulted in persecution, and, at times, in martyrdom.[135] Martyrdom itself was a contested category, but it is sufficient here to note that martyrs were bestowed with unique authority and favor. Christians executed by the Roman state were commonly thought to receive rewards in the afterlife; those who survived were accorded special authority in their worldly life.[136] Such proliferating authority figures pose a problem for Tertullian, who attempts to resolve it by using heresy to discipline the category of "martyr." In the end, he suggests the only real martyrs are those who subscribe to his version of Christianity.

Initially, Tertullian takes aim at the doctrines of Praxeas, a Christian teacher who viewed the godhead as an absolute unity and therefore indivisible into three entities (*Adv. Prax.* 1.1.1–2). According to Tertullian, incorrect doctrines like these exist because the devil opposes truth (*veritatem*) and, in this case, makes "heresy from the unity [of God]" (*haeresim*, at 1.1.1).[137] Praxeas is one of the devil's emissaries, responsible for spreading heresies to Rome (1.1.4). Despite holding diabolically incorrect views about God, though, Praxeas manages to manipulate the bishop of Rome. In fact, Praxeas convinced the bishop to rescind written recognition that leaders of the New Prophecy are blessed with divine gifts (1.1.5). The New Prophecy emphasized prophecy, revelation, and asceticism, and was later branded a heresy. Tertullian's degree of affiliation with the movement is unclear.[138] He certainly displays sympathies in *Adv. Prax.* In 1.1.5, Tertullian says Praxeas expels prophecy and introduces heresy (*haeresim*).[139] Praxeas' teachings regarding the unity of God are delegitimized as demonic subversion of orthodoxy.

The larger problem of religious authority cannot be resolved by simply labeling Praxeas a "heretic." This particular heretic is also a martyr (*martyrii*, 1.1.4), meaning his heresy could be legitimized via a martyr's special status.[140] To remedy this, Tertullian denies Praxeas' claim to being a martyr at all, first by trivializing his incarceration and then by claiming the man would not have received a martyr's rewards even if he had been executed (1.1.4). Praxeas excluded himself from God's love when he denied the legitimacy of prophecy, Tertullian claims (1.1.4–5). All of Praxeas' teachings must be suspect since he does not enjoy the love of God. As a result, Tertullian's criticism of Praxeas' influence over the bishop of Rome takes on greater urgency (1.1.4–5). This text heavily implies that the bishop heeded Praxeas because of the latter's status as martyr. Combining a rigidly disciplined label of heresy against certain martyrs allows Tertullian to pull a clever rhetorical maneuver: He makes the New

---

[135] Moss details the Roman evidence: 2012, pp. 9–12.   [136] Moss, 2010, pp. 16–17, 113–147.
[137] Latin from Evans, 1948, p. 89.   [138] Nasrallah, 2003, p. 100; cf., Dunn, 2004b, p. 4.
[139] Evans, 1948, p. 89.   [140] Evans, 1948, p. 89.

Prophecy orthodox since the bishop of Rome only de-recognized it because he had been manipulated by the heretic and false martyr, Praxeas. This further preserves the bishop of Rome's authority by blaming Praxeas, not the bishop, for the expulsion of prophecy. Tertullian can therefore insist that New Prophecy is orthodox without directly maligning the bishop of Rome. Tertullian ultimately declares that not all martyrs are authoritative. Indeed, not all of them are martyrs, even. Some are simply heretics, no matter what they experience at the hands of empire.

The aftermath of persecution also inflects the writings of Cyprian (d. 258 CE). Cyprian deploys *haeresis* to solidify his own authority as bishop over and against rival church leaders – a seemingly urgent issue after the first empire-wide persecution under Decius in 250 CE.[141] Cyprian guides his flock through this persecution, conducting business via a series of letters transmitted through his subordinates.[142] These letters suggest a community ruined by fragmentation and chaos after the Decian persecution. To center his own authority among competing claimants, Cyprian maps a reductive "insider versus outsider" binary onto multiple strategies for reintegrating lapsed Christians. He uses heresy to delegitimate competing modes of reintegration in order to centralize religious authority in the office of bishop.

When the Decian Persecution ends, Cyprian and his fellow clergy must wrestle with how to handle Christians who had apostatized to varying degrees and who now wished to be reconciled, that is, the "lapsed."[143] He advances a moderating position, claiming the lapsed can be reconciled after their case has been considered by the bishop and after they offer appropriate penance.[144] But other leaders, (including some martyrs) offered different solutions, from so-called "laxists" who did not require penance to "rigorists" who only offered reconciliation upon death, if then.[145] Much to Cyprian's displeasure, these diverging views led to the formation of rival leaders and congregations.

In a bid to reassert his own religious authority, Cyprian appeals to unity and to apostolic succession. "Heresies and schisms … undermine faith, corrupt truth, and rip apart unity," he says (*haereses*, at *De Unit.* 3).[146] Cyprian's demand for unity elides theological differences by subsuming them all under a generalizing abstraction. Rival leaders, despite being viewed as authoritative by their followers, do not have the authority to prescribe remedies for lapsed Christians.[147] All of these leaders are heretics simply by virtue of breaking with the unified

---

[141] Rives, 1999, pp. 135–137. On Cyprian's heresiologican ideation: Dunn, 2004a.
[142] Brendt, 2009, p. 8.   [143] Brendt, 2009, pp. 8–9.   [144] Brendt, 2009, p. 9.
[145] Brendt, 2009, pp. 10–11.   [146] Latin from CCSL 3.1, p. 211.
[147] Particularly in the case of Lucianus and Celerinus who were martyrs, insofar as they "confessed" and faced possible execution: Brendt, 2009, pp. 9–10.

church (i.e., Cyprian's orthodoxy). Cyprian uses *haeresis* in wide-ranging ways to substantiate such a generalizing claim. Heresy includes those who promise lapsed Christians easy reconciliation. Their congregations are a "heretical faction" (*haereticae factioni*, at *Ep.* 43.7.2).[148] So too are those who exclude repentant lapsed Christians *haeretici* (*Ep.* 55.27.1).[149] Rites like baptisms conducted "outside" the communion of the church are "heretical baptisms" (*de haereticorum baptismo*, at *Ep.* 73.1.1).[150] Finally, Cyprian repeatedly claims heretics are outsiders who willfully and maliciously deviate from orthodox unity (*Ep.* 55.27.1; 59.5.2; 59.18.1; 69.4.2; 70.3.2; 73.1.1).

Mapping an insider/outsider binary onto the categories of orthodoxy and heresy is a familiar rhetorical strategy, one especially prominent in heresiologies. Cyprian's writings buttress this binary via appeal to ecclesiastical hierarchies. Like Ignatius, he says heresy proliferates when people do not obey their bishop (*Ep.* 58.5.1).[151] This is because anyone who sets himself up as bishop does not derive his legitimacy from apostolic succession (*Ep.* 73.8.2; 73.14.3). Cyprian takes the rigidly disciplined category of heresy and combines it with another disciplining discourse – that pertaining to apostolic succession. Cyprian and others who remain united in obedience to the bishop are the true inheritors of apostolic legacy. He can thus position himself as an insider who has the religious authority to identify outsiders to orthodoxy. Still, we should take note: Cyprian may label all his rivals as willful and malicious heretics external to his unified apostolic orthodoxy, but their very existence indicates that the authority of bishops was not as secure as he would have us believe.

Tertullian and Cyprian are not representative of all third-century Christianities, of course. Different writers will deploy the category of heresy for different ends. Still, I think the writings of these two Carthaginian bishops offer a metonymy for broader discursive developments in this period. Specifically, we can see how heresy, having acquired its rigidly disciplined meaning, offers a ready-made way to police religious authority and deny it to those deemed heretics, whether they be martyrs or bishops.

Magic, Miracle, and Ascendant Christianity

By the second century, μαγεία/*magia* settles more firmly into its role as a marker of religious transgression.[152] This becomes a problem for Christianity. The broader move toward criminalizing magic means Christian authors had to wrestle with received legacies of wonderworking as well as wonderworking's role in propelling Christianity's ascendancy. We know that Christian writers

---
[148] CESL 3.2, p. 597.   [149] CESL 3.2, p. 644.   [150] CESL 3.2, p. 778.
[151] CESL 3.2, p. 671–672.   [152] Stratton, 2007, pp. 108–112.

ultimately created a new class of wonderworking – what we now know as miracle. But the question of what constitutes magic versus miracle is an internal one. That is, we cannot be sure non-Christians would have made the same distinctions. Evidence suggests the opposite is true: Christians were accused of using magic. Two very different texts demonstrate the same preoccupations with magic and its potential confusion with miracle: the apocryphal *Acts of Thomas* (*Acts Thom.*) and Origen's *Contra Celsum* (*C. Cels.*). Despite their seeming heterodoxy, both anticipate the notions of magic we find in Augustine and contemporaries.

The apocryphal *Acts Thom.* was composed in Syriac early in the third-century CE and translated into Greek not long after.[153] It features a highly fantastical narrative of the apostle Thomas' mission in India that advances an ascetic orthodoxy especially concerned with dietary restraint and chastity.[154] *Acts Thom.* may show Thomas performing wonders, but it fully denies the applicability of magic to Thomas' wonders. Accusations of magic only come from antagonists who are led by their decidedly un-ascetic passions and who therefore wish to destroy Thomas and his Christianity.

Foremost among Thomas' detractors is the Indian king, Misdaeus, who repeatedly calls the apostle a magician or magic-user (μάγος, at 104.1; μαγεύει, at 152.3) and further accuses Thomas of using potions to bewitch followers (φάρμακα, at 127.4, 163.12–13). Misdaeus is both rageful and lustful. He violences and imprisons Thomas to soothe petty personal grievances (138.12–13).[155] Misdaeus even threatens to imprison his own queen if she continues seeing that "magician" (μάγος, at 152.3). The king may have a towering rage, but he is weak-willed. One of his relatives, a man named Charisius, easily sways him to move against Thomas (99.4). Misdaeus is also hypocritical. For instance, he fears drowning in a flood that the Christian God sends to protect Thomas from being executed by burning. Although he gave the orders for Thomas' execution, Misdaeus commands the apostle to intercede with God on his behalf (140.11–141.1). Once he is spared, though, Misdaeus does not in turn spare Thomas (163.1–2). Instead, he orders the apostle to be executed again so India might be rid of Thomas' supposed enchantments (φάρμακα, at 163.13). Only at the story's end does he relent, after the deceased apostle's bones heal his son (170.8). Like Misdaeus, Charisius also accuses Thomas of being a μάγος (96.2, 101.3–6, 102.3).[156] Also like the king, Charisius is driven by the things Thomas counsels against. Specifically, he is

---

[153] Schneemelcher, 2003, p. 323.   [154] Schneemelcher, 2003, pp. 325–327.
[155] Greek from Bonnet, 1903: μάγος, p. 216; μαγεύει, p. 261; φάρμακα: p. 235 and pp. 275–276, respectively.
[156] Bonnet, 1903, p. 209, pp. 213–214, and p. 215, respectively.

in lust with his wife, Mygdonia. When she converts and so refuses fine clothes, lavish food, and sex (96.3, 99.1), Charisius tries to sway her from Thomas and his "deeds of magic" (ἔργοις τῆς μαγείας, at 96.4).[157] Her refusal is taken as a personal insult, and Charisius cruelly states that he would prefer Mygdonia to die a violent death than persist in her association with Thomas (100.3).

The *Acts Thom.* uses characterization to launch its critique of those who might accuse Christians of using magic. Misdaeus and Charisius are foils for Thomas' asceticism, true. But they also work as "stand-ins" for non-Christians who might levy accusations of magic. Juxtapose these two men with associates of another Indian king in 20.1. These others offer the following report on Thomas' missionary work: He travels, preaches a new God, cares for the poor, and performs healings, exorcisms, and other wonders (20.1). "We suppose he is a magician," they initially say (καὶ νομίζομεν ἡμεῖς ὅτι μάγος ἐστίν, 20.1).[158] But they revise this assessment almost immediately: "... his compassion, and the healings which he does freely, signify his sincerity and the kindness of his faith (20.2)." Thomas' simplicity and morality preclude an accusation of magic early in the *Acts Thom.* Later, when the hotheaded Misdaeus and the lustful Charisius accuse Thomas of using magic despite benefitting from the apostle's sincerity and kindness, the audience knows such accusations must be resultant of petty grievance rather than any real similarity between Thomas' miracles and mere magic. The audience would do well not to take such accusers at their word, our author seems to say.

In a different genre of text from this century, the great Alexandrian Church Father Origen (d. 253 CE) explicitly refutes an accusation of magic. Origen's *Contra Celsum* (*C. Cels.*) is a defense of Christianity against criticisms offered by an earlier second-century philosopher named Celsus. One of Celsus' many accusations involves Christians' use of magic (μαγείαν, at 1.68).[159] To refute this charge, Origen concedes that Christian wonderworking certainly resembles the wares peddled by sorcerers in the marketplace (1.6). He states outright that miracles helped establish Christianity (2.51). But there are key differences between Christian miracle and others' magic: (1) Christians use only the name of Jesus (1.6); and (2) miracles engender moral reformation (6.39). In sum, Christians have nothing at all to do with magic (μαγείᾳ, at 6.41).[160]

Origen is not the only Christian writer who appeals to the relatively simple nature of Christian wonderworking; others make the same distinctions between things like Christian exorcistic formulae and more elaborate magical ones.[161]

---

[157] Bonnet, 1903, p. 209. [158] Bonnet, 1903, p. 131.
[159] Greek from GCS: Koetschau, 1899a, pp. 121–122.
[160] GCS, Koetschau, 1899b, pp. 109–110.
[161] Tertullian, *Apol.* 23. Discussed in Proctor, 2022, pp. 108–114.

But as Travis W. Proctor shows, simple formulae exist in wider Greco-Roman literature.[162] Origen and others who appeal to simplicity create a practical difference between miracle and magic that is unsustainable when we consider extant historical evidence. That said, *C. Cels.* also refutes accusations of magic along "interiorized" indices like morality and epistemic superiority.[163] Jesus' miracles – and by extension, those of other Christians – not only heal the body, they can heal the soul (1.9). These wonders turn those who receive them toward God (6.39). Additionally, Christian miracles come from a secure epistemic source. According to Origen, Jesus secretly disseminated many things to his followers, including a "certain power" that imparted true knowledge (1.31). This power not only helps transmit the correct teachings, but it also drives healings, exorcisms, and certain types of divination (1.46). Since this power is handed down by Jesus and given only to Christians, marketplace magicians cannot access it. Instead, magicians are shameful and sinful, unconcerned with morality (1.68), and draw their power from evil demons (2.51). For all these reasons, "there are no magicians who work under the pretense of a religion of this [moral] character" (τοὺς μαγγανεύοντας προφάσει τῆς κατὰ τὸν χαρακτῆρα τοῦτον θεοσεβείας, 6.39).[164] Notice how Origen places the onus of differentiation on an observer. Sure, the two may look alike, but magic and miracle represent two fundamentally different "species" (2.51), he says. The implication is that a keen observer would not be fooled by superficial similarities.

The *Acts Thom.* and *C. Cels.* come from very different genres and advance distinct orthodoxies. But both appear to share anxieties that many Christian writers of this period navigated. The increasing visibility of Christianity and its wonderworking legacy, coupled with more prevalent uses of magic to signify religious deviance, demanded a broad refutation of magic. No longer content to limit their deflections to specific practices or to practitioners like magician-heresiarchs, these texts discredit magic as such, either by characterizing accusers as petty and spiteful (*Acts Thom.*) or by marking difference along interiorized lines that allow for superficial similarities between magic and miracle (*C. Cels.*).

This section's case study, the *Refutation against All Heresies*, exemplifies what happens when third-century views of magic meet contemporaneous views of heresy. This text also appears to be concerned with accusations of magic being levied at Christianity. To deflect them, it uses rigidly disciplined views of heresy as marking theological outsiders coupled with views of magic as morally and epistemically inferior to a Christianity that seems rather lacking in wonders.

---

[162] Proctor, 2022, pp. 108–114.   [163] Gallagher, 1982, pp. 59–61.
[164] Koetschau, 1899b, p. 108.

Case Study: Hippolytus' Refutation of All Heresies

The *Refutation of All Heresies* is a heresiological text attributed to Hippolytus of Rome (d. ca. 235-6 CE). Here, we learn of magician-heresiarchs familiar to us from earlier texts. Like their predecessors, the teachings and wonders of these figures are little more than cheap trickery designed to deceive the masses.[165] The *Refutation* layers its heresiological ideation with a kind of apologia designed to insulate its orthodoxy from being confused for magic. According to M. David Litwa, this text's overarching purpose lies in exposing supposed heretics (αἱρετικῶν, at 1.1.1) as plagiarists who lift ideas from Greek philosophers, mysteries, and astrologers (1.1.1–8).[166] Book IV, the subject of this study, takes specific aim at "magical deeds" (μάγων ἔργα), which our author characterizes as deceits heretics use to prey upon the ignorant (4.42.1). Hippoloytus, like Celsus, launches a dual attack against magician-heresiarchs that delegitimizes the epistemic origins of supposed heresies alongside their magic.

Hippolytus tackles practical facets of magic in 4.28–42, a section that reads like an exposé of the sorts of parlor tricks that constitute magic. So, for instance, 4.35.3 relates the following procedure for faking epiphanies: "[The magician] makes a demon catch fire by forming on the wall the desired shape. Then he secretly anoints himself with a potion (φαρμάκῳ) .... Then, as [if pretending to be] inspired, he brings the lamp to the wall, and the potion sparks and catches fire." Similarly, the *Refutation* exposes behind-the-scenes machinery for divination (4.28, 35, 40), conjuring natural phenomena (4.32.1, 39), manipulating fire (4.31, 32.2–33.1), summoning divine entities (4.35.4–5, 37), and other rituals that are described as "magical deeds" in 4.42.1. In laying bare magicians' cheap ruses, Hippolytus disillusions the audience. These, and "ten thousand other tricks like them," are fabricated by heretics who use them to mislead unwitting followers (4.42.1) – the implication being that those who *are* convinced must indeed be ignorant.

Despite finding nothing of substance in magical deeds, Hippolytus grants their allure. Early on, he describes how a great many people incorrectly assume that heretics (αἱρετικῶν) worship God (θεὸν σέβειν) (1.1.1). Revealing these supposed heretics' professional secrets exposes how these figures get confused for worshippers of God (1.1.1–8). In this way, Hippolytus can also issue a warning to self-professed Christians who patronize magicians. Though alluring, wonders are the tacky artifice of "heretics, [who,] having been awed by [magicians'] art, imitated it ... paraphrasing [magicians'] teachings as if their own" (ὧν τὴν τέχνην

---

[165] Authorship is debated, but the third-century date is more secure. Authorship is not our primary concern, so I refer to our author as "Hippolytus." Discussion in Litwa, 2016, xxvii–xxviii.

[166] Litwa, *Refutation*, xlii–xliii.

καταπλαγέντες οἱ αἱρεσιάρχαι ἐμιμήσαντο … τὸ δὲ καὶ παραφράζοντες ὡς ἴδια, 4.42.1). Magic is a "foreign" imposition, shallow and counterfeit, perhaps worthless even to those who use it (4.42.3). Sure, magician-heretics attract the more gullible of the masses, but they can never offer truth. They do not worship God. Whatever knowledge they possess is plagiarized from corrupt epistemic sources. Hippolytus' exposé makes magic part of the secret knowledge that allows magician-heresiarchs to be misidentified as Christians. Now that Hippolytus has exposed how magic works, and how mundane it truly is, the audience can recognize magician-heresiarchs for the fraudulent, plagiarizing deceivers they are. We also have here another explanation for accusations of magic against Christians. But instead of acknowledging superficial similarities between magic and miracle like Origen and *Acts Thom.*, Hippolytus suggests that anyone accusing Christians of magic must surely be confusing the tawdry tricks of heretics for true worship of the Christian God.

Coda: The Empire against Christianity

Third-century Christianities may have had increased visibility, but their ascendancy brought a number of problems that required our authors, proto-orthodox or not, to assume a defensive posture. Sites of imperial scrutiny like persecutions or formal and informal accusations of magic provided new conceptual terrain where writers combine multiple disciplining discourses to insulate and strengthen their respective orthodoxies. Both Tertullian and Cyprian use *haeresis* to legitimate the office of the bishop while simultaneously delegitimating martyrological authorities. Both presuppose a cohesive community from which heretics depart. And finally, both depend on the disciplining function of heresy to advance their own theological and ecclesiastical projects. Tertullian insists that the New Prophecy is legitimate precisely because it was de-recognized through a heretic's manipulation. Cyprian, for his part, claims methods of reintegrating lapsed believers that do not align with his own are heretical. Their arguments work if one accepts their premise that religious authority resides in the office of the bishop. Heresy here is used to sustain proto-orthodox church hierarchies. With respect to magic, these same historical pressures prompt more urgent distancing of Christianity and magic. Third-century authors appeal to the strong notion of magic, disciplined now to mark religious deviance. Magic is overwhelmingly pejorative, but this provides generative conceptual foils for many Christian writers of this period: Magic is avaricious, immoral, and nothing but smoke and mirrors. In contrast, the Christianities we encounter are simple and sincere, aimed at prompting moral reformation, and transmitting edifying truth.

The third century increases the conceptual distance between Christianity and magic and Christianity and heresy. Naturally, this demands erasure or elision of inconvenient historical facts. Consider again Origen, who ties himself into rhetorical knots when trying to explain why "evil men" can successfully use Jesus' name to effect wonders (*C. Cels.* 1.6).[167] Betraying his insistent differentiation, however, is the inconvenient fact that marketplace sorcerers (said "evil men") apparently did not recognize or did not care to make the same distinctions between magic and Christian miracle. Other contemporary notions of heresy and magic also hint at the sorts of negotiations writers made between an ascendant Christianity and the Roman Empire. To be clear: By "Roman empire," I mean both geopolitical entity and discursive construct. The *Acts Thom.* for instance does not initially appear to be a response to Roman cultural forms. It takes place in faraway India. But Thomas' Indian interlocutors reflect reigning Roman stereotypes of magic as greedy and deceptive. This is why the apostle's simple and sincere ministry cannot be magic (*Acts Thom.* 20.1–2). Even exoticized foreigners can see the difference between magic and Christianity, the text seems to assert. Tertullian and Cyprian contend with the machinery of the state. Both impart, intentionally or unintentionally, how persecution by imperial authorities causes chaos within Christian communities. This pair of Carthaginian bishops centers developing ecclesiastical hierarchies in the face of competing authority claims from martyrs, the latter of whom proliferate in the literary record even though, historically, Roman persecution of Christians was sporadic and short-lived.[168] Surprisingly charismatic martyrs produced by the imposition of imperial power do not, by default, have religious authority. The fact that Tertullian and Cyprian felt compelled to exclude martyrs implies that martyrs were perceived as a possible threat to developing church hierarchies in this period. Christianity's ascendancy within the broader matrix of Roman religious and epistemic systems was not without its own crises.

Any crises do not linger long. In merely a few decades after the close of the third century, Christianity will reside at the epicenter of the Roman Empire. The ascendant imperial religion will once again redefine itself to accommodate new realities as well as its new role. Authors will create totalizing epistemic regimes wherein they deploy magic and heresy in order to position their orthodoxy as eternally sovereign and supreme. So emerges the late ancient épistémè I discussed in the introductory section. Once forged, this épistémè demands a classification of all religious and epistemic systems and their related phenomena as either (magic-)heresy or orthodoxy.

---

[167] Discussion in Gallagher, 1982, pp. 44–45.
[168] Moss distills the relevant evidence: 2012, pp. 8–16.

Totalizing Epistemologies and Imperial Orthodoxy: The Fourth Century

Discourses of αἵρεσις/*haeresis* and μαγεία/*magia* in the fourth-century CE initially seem like revivals of second-century heresiologies. But heresiological ideation changes shape in late antiquity, especially after imperial orthodoxy gets established as the religion of the Roman Empire. The discursive disciplining we saw earlier continues to hone magic and heresy into sharper rhetorical weapons better suited for a contemporaneous context. And the literary architects of imperial orthodoxy we meet in this section have benefitted from previous cycles of discursive disciplining. From second-century heresiologies, they inherit overwhelmingly pejorative notions of magic and heresy. Magician-heresiarchs still haunt texts from this period, but they are not the only ones guilty of magic-heresy. In fact, both categories expand and ultimately overlap until the two are functionally coequal, meaning that all heresy is implicated in magic and that all magic is heretical by default. Very often, both αἵρεσις/*haeresis* and μαγεία/*magia* are invoked together, further evidencing how the conceptual associations created over the last few centuries have ossified to become part of a common cultural lexicon. Alongside their third-century counterparts, writers in this period seem profoundly aware of Christianity's visibility within the broader matrix of Roman religious and epistemic systems. Naturally, they are less preoccupied with real or perceived persecution, though Christianity still had to defend itself against accusations of magic even after becoming imperial religion.[169] Rather, fourth-century Christian writers create totalizing overlaps between magic and heresy, often by way of epistemology. Here, "epistemology" refers to both the source of an individual's knowledge as well as to the discernment of true from false knowledge. Perhaps this task is what prompts late ancient writers to adopt totalizing epistemologies. They position themselves as the ultimate knowers, of truth versus falsehood, sure, but they also presume or pretend to have knowledge about the beliefs and practices of groups deemed heretical. What finally emerges is a notion of Christianity as having always been free from the influence of magic-heresy. Our case study, Eusebius of Caesarea's (d. 339 CE) *Ecclesiastical History* (*HE*) exemplifies this view of an eternal and transcendent orthodoxy that was destined to be superior and sovereign.

Before considering individual texts, I want to distill a major literary trend scholars have identified in Christian writings that lead up to its recognition as imperial religion in 380 CE. Decades beforehand, Christians started writing about themselves differently.[170] This is especially true after Christianity starts receiving

---

[169] For example, Augustine's defense of Christianity: *Cons. Ev.* 1.10.15; *Contra Faust.* 29; discussion and evidence in Kahlos, 2019, p. 198, n. 20.

[170] Cameron, 1994, pp. 120–141, at p. 122; Jacobs, 2004, pp. 21.

patronage from Emperor Constantine I (d. 337 CE).[171] A heightened emphasis on epistemology emerges from these new modes of self-definition prompted by new relationships to empire. Christians' preoccupation with knowledge and meaning-making gets expressed in two ways: (1) a positioning of the author as knower and arbiter of truth, that is, of orthodoxy; and (2) the imposition of a paradoxically totalizing and reductive historiographical gaze that arranges the cosmos into a rigid binary between truth (i.e., orthodoxy), on the one hand, and magic-heresy, on the other.[172] In the end, totalizing epistemologies demand totalizing understandings of both magic and heresy, since both discourses facilitate Christian self-definition. No wonder, then, that the two categories seem rather abstract in the following texts – no longer as unwieldy or contradictory as they once were, but unnuanced rhetorical weapons against *all* rivals. Functionally, this makes magic and heresy coequal.

Heresy and Totalizing Epistemologies

One way late ancient writers apply a totalizing epistemology involves constructing a historiographical narrative stretching back into mythic history, to events and to knowledge an ordinary Roman could not acquire. These authors construct a rigid conceptual binary between truth and error, the latter of which results from bad or corrupted knowledge. Such rhetorical strategies are prescriptive in that they are designed to instruct the audience about where to find epistemic certainty or truth. Particularly fascinating is the fact that these rhetorical strategies obtain in texts that do not strictly represent imperial orthodoxy, suggesting that the conflation magic-heresy was in the water, so to speak.

One writer who appeals to and helps reify a totalizing epistemology is Epiphanius of Salamis (d. 403 CE). Epiphanius' *Panarion* (*Pan.*) is ostensibly a catalog of all heresies (αἱρέσεων) as well as an intellectual "cure" for refuting them (*Proem* 1.1).[173] His encyclopedic presentation of heresies authorizes Epiphanius as someone with enough knowledge to essay such a catalog in the first place.[174] *Pan.* begins by claiming that epistemic and religious systems classed as heresies originated in five "mother [heresies]," with each giving rise to whole cascades of heresies, past and present.[175] Mother heresies correspond to phases in cosmic history; Epiphanius names them "Barbarism," "Scythianism," "Hellenism," "Judaism," and "Samaritanism" (*Proem* 3.1). The first, Barbarism, spans from Creation to the biblical Flood (1.1.1). During this era, "wickedness" enters the

---

[171] Jacobs, 2004, p. 21.
[172] Discussion of this totalizing discourse and cognitive control in Jacobs, 2004, pp. 21–32, esp. the examples on p. 24.
[173] Greek from GCS: Holl, 1915, p. 169.   [174] Flower, 2010, pp. 70–87.
[175] Schott, 2007, p. 548; Flower, 2010.

world through the descendants of Adam, causing God to send the Flood as a righteous judgment (1.1.3–6). But even as Barbarianism witnessed the rise of enchantment (φαρμακεία), magic (μαγεία), lawlessness, adultery, and unrighteousness (1.1.3), there was no "heterodoxy" (ἑτεροδοξία) and no "name for heresy" (ὄνομα αἱρέσεως) (1.1.9).[176] In other words, earliest heresy is not dependent upon recognized groups or the false teachings of a demonolatrous magician-heresiarch. Rather, all the world's transgressions originated in the "evil teachings" (κακῆς διδαχῆς) of magic (μαγείας) and astrology (ἀστρολογίας) (1.3.3).[177] This, then, gives the audience an interpretive framework for assessing religious and epistemic systems: They either originate in magic-heresy, or in something else.

In locating the origin of heresy in the mythic past, *Pan.* advances several rhetorical strategies. First, Epiphanius positions himself as a knower, one who has specialized knowledge of the primeval past, even. The text thus implies that an audience can take his word about the heresies he subsequently catalogs.[178] Second, this totalizing historiography allows *Pan.* to posit an eternal enemy that was always arrayed against an eternal and transcendent truth. When discussing the second stage of cosmic history – Scythianism – Epiphanius clarifies that "piety and impiety, faith and faithlessness, were working then" (1.2.7). These early forms of piety and faith were precursors to the present-day church (1.2.4) and to "Christianity" (Χριστιανισμοῦ, at 1.2.7).[179] So, all forms of piety and faithfulness are essentially Christian. Christianity is not subject to historical change.[180] Its religious or epistemic competitors, in contrast, come from enchantment, magic, and lawlessness.

Though sometimes marginalized in modern scholarship, Epiphanius was one of many thinkers who helped write and maintain imperial orthodoxy.[181] But even supposedly heterodox texts of this period adopt totalizing epistemologies like the one found in *Pan.* Take the Pseudo-Clementine *Homilies* (*Hom.*) for instance. This text(s) draws upon the same Jewish pseudepigraphic traditions as *Pan.*[182] The final, fourth-century redaction was once overlooked in scholarship because it reflects a "Jewish-Christianity" that was thought to wane in influence by late antiquity.[183] Although *Hom.* defines its orthodoxy differently from Epiphanius, the Homilist retains totalizing epistemologies to accomplish similar heresiological ends as *Pan.*[184]

---

[176] Holl, 1915, pp. 172–173.   [177] Holl, 1915, p. 177.   [178] Flower, 2010, pp. 70–87.
[179] Holl, 1915, p. 175.   [180] Schott, 2007, p. 547.
[181] Discussion of secondary scholarship and Epiphanius' influence: Kim, 2015, pp. 1–8 and Jacobs, 2021, pp. 1–13.
[182] Review of scholarship in Kelley, 2006, pp. 17–27.
[183] On modern scholarship and the "Jewish-Christianity" of the *Homilies*: Reed, 2003, esp. pp. 197–201 and 2008, pp. 273–276.
[184] On *Hom.* as heresiology comparable to *Pan.*, see Reed, 2008, esp. pp. 283–288.

On its surface, the *Homilies* is a forged autobiographical account of Clement of Rome, who meets the apostle Peter and accompanies him on a missionary journey. Much like Epiphanius, the Homilist gazes back into mythic history and constructs two separate lineages for good and bad knowledge, represented respectively by Peter and Simon of Samaria. Simon uses magic to gather followers, but *Hom.* is clear about where magic comes from in sections 8.12–14. In mythic history, angels lusted after human women and became demons on account (8.12). When asked to show their previous angelic forms, they could no longer do so (8.14). Instead, they distracted their human lovers with forbidden knowledge of precious metals, magical stones, magic (μαγείαν), and astrology (8.14). Unfortunately, though, this knowledge takes on a life of its own, giving rise to the religious and epistemic systems of the Egyptians, Persians, and Babylonians (8.17), Greco-Roman philosophy (1.3), paganisms (9.6), and, in its characterization of Simon, to all other Christianities as well.[185] In this schema, Simon is still a magician-heresiarch who uses magic to preach heresies (αἱρέσεις), ones that will linger well into the future, according to the Homilist (16.21). For his part, Peter preaches an unadulterated and eternal truth (19.3). Before the angels fell, before demonic knowledge created so many epistemic rivals, the truth was revealed to Adam in Eden (8.10). Since then, it has remained uncorrupted because it is painstakingly preserved in Jewish writings and rituals and is only disseminated via tightly controlled lines of transmission (2.38; 3.41).[186] The *Hom.* claims Jesus is one of many True Prophets appointed by God to preach truth. Peter receives knowledge directly from Jesus and he is careful never to change what he learned (19.2). So, when the Homilist reproduces Petrine teachings in a series of lengthy sermons that monopolize the narrative, a reader ought to view his teachings as conveying truth.[187] Conversely, any external knowledge comes from the same heretical epistemic lineage as Simon, one rooted in the demonic knowledge of magic.

As with Epiphanius, the Clementine *Homilies* adopts a totalizing historiographical gaze to classify every religious and epistemic system into two separate epistemic lineages: that of truth or of heresy originating in magical knowledge. Both texts suggest that heresy has always been opposed to an eternal and transcendent orthodoxy. Christianity has never had anything to do with magic, they assert.

Totalizing epistemologies appear in monastic texts, too. In the late fourth-century *Historia Monachorum in Aegypto* (*HM*), the author(s) adopt a different rhetorical strategy to frame their totalizing worldview. The *HM* relies on an

---

[185] Côté, 2001 and 2012, pp. 191–196.
[186] On "oral-aural" revelation: Han, 2023, pp. 141–146. [187] Reed, 2008, p. 287.

historical event – the Christianization of Egypt – to authorize its knowledge. This text narrates the fantastical events experienced by a group of Christians traveling through Egypt.[188] One of the monks we meet is Apollo, a charismatic wonder-worker who Christianizes all of Egypt with his spectacular miracles. His mission is described in the following manner: "Through [Apollo], [the Lord] will destroy the wisdom of wise Egyptians and will bring to naught the intelligence of intelligent pagans ... [Apollo] will destroy the wise Babylonians and [he] will eradicate all worship of demons ..." (8.3). Here, Jesus himself tasks Apollo with destroying the religious and epistemic systems of the Egyptians, Babylonians, and all paganisms besides. The *HM* authorizes itself via etiology: Apollo's miracles explain the widespread Christianization of Egypt, particularly its monasticization.[189] Naturally, not every Egyptian will have converted, but *HM* leaves no room for the survival of local religions, claiming that all temples were converted to monasteries and that Egypt was overrun with monastics (5.2; 8.20). No heretic or pagan could be found anywhere – such was the power of Apollo's miracle-driven ministry (5.4). *HM*'s historiographical gaze is more limited than those of Epiphanius and the Homilist, but it is still totalizing. Potential adherents have a choice between Christianity or heresy. This conceptual binary is strengthened by *HM*'s concomitant expansion of heresy to encompass non-Christians. Our author conflates heresy with "Greeks" (Ἕλληνες), a category that grew to denote all non-Christians in a generalizing fashion.[190]

These texts represent different Christian orthodoxies but they adopt a totalizing epistemology that helps to expand the category of heresy. In these fourth-century CE texts, heresy covers all religious and epistemic rivals to authors' respective orthodoxies. This is quite a shift from first-century notions of heresy that applied the label in more limited ways, as a means of describing sects within early communities of Christ-believers or as designating a choice between eschatological options. Now, heresy can apply to every religious and epistemic other that was, is, or will ever be. And no matter the Christianity under examination, its orthodoxy is always external and opposed to heresy.

Magic and Imperial Orthodoxy

If heresy expands by way of late ancient Christians' totalizing epistemologies, so too does μαγεία/*magia*. In heresiological texts, magic was a tool for magician-heresiarchs to deceive followers. Third-century Christian literature distances magic and Christianity. By the fourth century, magic has already become

---

[188] Cain, 2016, p. 1.   [189] Cain, 2016, pp. 186–187.
[190] Cain, 2016, p. 183; citing Gregory of Nyssa, *C. Eun.* 3.2.72; Gregory of Nazianzus, *Orat.* 38.2; Cyril of Jerusalem, *Cat.* 8.1. For the slippage between "heretic" and "pagan": Schroeder, 2007, pp. 131–139.

a kind of epistemology – a bad or corrupted knowledge. However, the totalizing epistemologies so prevalent in Christian writings from this period make magic even more expansive and abstract. Religious othering via accusations of magic results in the same paradoxically totalizing and reductive conceptual binaries as the applications of heresy we see in the aforementioned texts.

Consider a series of virulently Judeophobic sermons by John Chrysostom (d. 407 CE), now known as *Against the Jews* (*Adv. Iud.*). These homilies were preached between 386–387 CE and were directed toward members of the church of Antioch who were deemed "Judaizers" – that is, Christians who adhered to facets of Jewish religion and practice, like observing certain festivals and fasts (*Adv. Iud.* 3.4.3; 1.4.7).[191] One of the many Judaizing tendencies that provoked our author's ire involved congregants seeking curatives from Jewish ritual experts. Chrysostom uses magic to demonize the ritual experts in question, but then he extends his criticism to Judaism as such. In so doing, he strengthens associations between Judaism and magic.

Magic enters the picture in *Adv. Iud.* 8. Chrysostom rails against Christians who seek out therapeutics for everyday ailments like pain or fever. He calls these remedies "magic tricks" (μαγγανείας, at 8.6.6).[192] Additionally, he stacks practices and accoutrements regularly stereotyped as magical to further describe the aforementioned tricks: They are "spells" (ἐπῳδάς), "amulets" (περιάμματα), and "potions" (φαρμακείας) (8.5.6).[193] Later, Chrysostom cautions his followers not to run to synagogues or call upon sorcerers (γόητας) who trade in such tricks (μαγγανείας) (8.6.6).[194] While these additional terms are beyond the scope of this volume, I want to note how the accrual of this vocabulary intensifies the accusation of magic. There is little room here to view these activities as non-magical.

Already, we should note Chrysostom's implication that sorcerers lurk in synagogues, waiting to sell their magical wares to gullible Christians. In *Adv. Iud.* 8.8.4, he claims that he has spoken to some Jewish experts who say demons can effect cures (θεραπεύοσι δαίμονες, at 8.8.4).[195] Chrysostom's appeal to Jewish use of demons adopts popular stereotypes of magicians using *demons* as helpers or *parhedroi*.[196] In Roman polytheisms, demons were intermediary beings who could cause good or ill effects, but such neutral or ambiguous evaluations of these entities cannot obtain here. For Chrysostom, they are diabolical – indicated by his breezy conflation of demons with "devil" in the

---

[191] On dating: Harkins, 1979, pp. xii–xxv. Audience: Harkins, 1979, pp. xxvi–xxvii. Contra Harkins, I retain the title *Against the Jews*, since I argue that Chrysostom demonizes all Jews even if his immediate audience might be Judaizing Christians.
[192] Online LSJ: https://lsj.gr/wiki/μαγγανεία. [193] PG 48.935.19–20. [194] PG 48.936.42–43.
[195] PG 48.940.21-2. [196] Gordon, 1999, pp. 182–188.

very next line (8.8.4). Jewish ritual experts might assert that demons help them heal, but Christ warned Christians that the devil (διάβολου) has always been a murderer (8.8.4).[197] Why, then, would a good Christian seek healings from demonolatrous Jews, Chrysostom wonders (8.8.4). He eventually makes the audacious claim that simply entering a synagogue makes one susceptible to demonic influence (8.8.7). Chrysostom implies that demons used by Jewish ritual experts make synagogues a site of evil demonic contagion – a move that demonizes all synagogues and Judaism by extension. In *Adv. Iud.* 8.6.11, he goes further and asserts that all Jewish people use spells (ἐπῳδαῖς).[198] Chrysostom tethers this magic-laden Judaism to heresy. Jews are beyond forgiveness and completely cut off from God, he asserts (8.6.11). Even if Jewish experts claim to heal fevers with spells, they can only cause harm (8.6.11). Asking them for curatives violates a Christian's covenant with Christ (8.6.11).

Adv. Iud. 8 is a series of rhetorical sleights-of-hand that result in a totalizing conflation of magic and Judaism. Chrysostom begins by talking about specific curatives proffered by Jewish experts, to characterizing all Jews who cure as demonolatrous, to implying that demons reside in synagogues, to eventually demonizing all Jews. *Adv. Iud.* 8 clearly appropriates long-standing orientalized notions of Jews as being well-versed in certain magical practices.[199] But we have no evidence to confirm his assessment that the ritual experts in question self-identified as magicians or viewed their healings as magical. Even so, Chrysostom adopts a position of epistemic superiority, not only accusing ritual experts of being demonolatrous sorcerers, but claiming that all Jews use magic. In a sense, these rhetorical strategies place magic in conceptual opposition to Christianity, which is magicless.

Incidentally, Chrysostom does not seem to be averse to charms in general. Margaret M. Mitchell has argued that he creates his own charm against adultery, even using the term ἔπᾳδε ("sing an incantation"), which shares a root with the ἐπῳδαῖς he found so objectionable in *Adv. Iud* 8.6.11.[200] This inconsistency exposes his totalizing project: Wonders themselves matter less than wonder-workers' religious affiliation. Jews use demonic magic because they are cut off from God. We can assume Chrysostom's spell is not magic precisely because it advances good Christian virtues. An accusation of magic like this, one that demonizes an entire religious tradition, helps create totalizing overlaps between magic and heresy.

---

[197] PG 48.940.23–4.   [198] PG 48.937.35–43.
[199] Orientalization of magic: Gordon, 1999, pp. 191–194. See, too, the evidence in Wendt, 2016, pp. 87–91.
[200] *Hom. 1 Cor.* 7–4; Mitchell, 2022, p. 137. For Mitchell's translation of ἔπᾳδε, p. 137 n. 94.

The tendency to make magic coterminous with religious and epistemic rivals also appears in a late fourth-century hagiography written by Jerome (d. ca. 419–420 CE). The *Life of Hilarion* (*VH*) is a highly embellished biographical account of the monk Hilarion, a man who establishes Christianity throughout ancient Palestine.[201] The *VH* elevates its own orthodoxy by creating an overlap between magic and paganism. In 20, Hilarion attends horse races in Gaza. There, he is petitioned by a local Christian named Italicus, who beseeches the holy man for a miracle. Italicus' opponent, a pagan devotee of Marnas, has paid a sorcerer (*maleficus*) to ensure victory through the use of demonic incantations (*daemoniacis imprecationibus*) (20). Initially, Hilarion demurs, stating that he does not wish to waste his powerful prayers on games. Italicus prevails upon him, though, when he tells Hilarion that a Christian cannot employ "magical arts" (*magicis artibus*, at 20). Italicus must instead seek help from a servant of Christ (20).

Maijastina Kahlos sees in this exchange a clear divorcing of Christianity and magic.[202] I would add that *VH* also presupposes this conceptual divorce. Italicus cannot pay a sorcerer to ensure his victory because sorcerers use demonic incantations. He can, however, appeal to a servant of Christ for a prayerful miracle. But *VH* does more, too. Jerome makes the competition between Italicus and his pagan opponent into a full-scale religious rivalry. As he begs Hilarion for help, Italicus characterizes the crowd as enemies of God who insult the church of Christ (20). But when he wins, the same crowd interpret Italicus' victory as a triumph of Christ over Marnas (*Marnas victus est a Christo*, at 20). His embittered opponents accuse Hilarion of being a "Christian sorcerer" (*maleficum Christianum*, at 20) and attempt to have the monk executed, but they are the only ones who make this mistake. The spectators in *VH* 20 are an ideal audience: When they witness Hilarion's miracle, they recognize immediately that he is no magician. Moreover, they understand that Christianity is superior to paganism. Even though this scene does not appear to adopt a totalizing epistemology like others in this section, it represents a grand battle between Christianity and paganisms. "The circus was often conceived as a microcosm of the pagan world, and Jerome's Christian hero is thus defeating his opponents at the symbolic center of pagan urban life," writes Susan Weingarten.[203] Paganism and magic overlap in *VH* 20; the defeat of magical paganism results in the triumph of Christianity.

These three texts make magic the purview of rival religious or epistemic systems. Even when they start by criticizing individual practices or practitioners,

---

[201] Weingarten, 2005, p. 105.   [202] Kahlos, 2020, pp. 128–129.
[203] Weingarten, 2005, p. 107.

authors like Chrysostom and Jerome end up using magic to mark un-Christian individuals and practices. They can presuppose separation between magic and orthodoxy because magic had become a recognized means of signifying religious transgression by the fourth-century CE. But these authors also expand the category of magic, no longer a tool used by magician-heresiarchs, but a religious or epistemic system in its own right. At the very least, magic is conceptually weighty enough to be placed in apposition to Christianity as such.

Case Study: Eusebius' Ecclesiastical History

Perhaps it is fitting that we end this final section with Eusebius of Caesarea (d. ca. 339–340 CE) and *Ecclesiastical History* (*HE*). Eusebius was a critical figure in the development of imperial orthodoxy. He served as an adviser to Constantine I and played a major role at the Council of Nicaea in 325 CE.[204] *HE* purports to tell the complete history of Christianity, from its inception to Eusebius' day. According to the text, the true church has always remained faithful to the teachings Jesus that were passed down by the apostles; any heresies are derivative offshoots of original apostolic orthodoxy. Throughout, Eusebius combines discourses of magic and heresy in totalizing ways. Like his contemporaries, he develops divergent epistemic lineages for orthodoxy and heresy. Then, he makes his religious and epistemic competitors heresy. Magic is both a tool of heresiarchs and a heresy. In contrast, *HE*'s imperial orthodoxy is eternal and transcendent, and has always been free of magic-heresy.

Eusebius locates the origins of heresy in Simon of Samaria. The infamous magician-heresiarch was so enthralled by miracles that he "feigned his faith in Christ" (2.1.11).[205] *HE* accuses individuals who adhere to Simon's heresy (αἵρεσιν) of likewise counterfeiting their faith and worshipping demons (2.1.12). Heresies like Simon's arose because demons used the magician to thwart God (2.13.1–3). Even after Peter realized Simon's true nature and chastised him, heresies continue to proliferate (2.1.12). For instance, Simon has disciples like Menander, who also use magical arts (μαγικῆς τέχνης, at 3.27.4) to spread false doctrines (3.26.1). Although both men deceptively identify as "Christian," Eusebius thinks they defame the church via magic (μαγείᾳ, at 3.27.4). Here, we see how *HE* presupposes and further reifies the conceptual distance between magic-heresy and imperial orthodoxy.

Magic does more than make and mark heresy in *HE*, though. Eusebius uses it to create an interpretive paradigm for delegitimizing religious and epistemic

---

[204] Dating: Lake, 1926, p. xi.
[205] Eusebius uses μαγεία and γοητεία almost interchangeably, so Simon the magician (μάγον) is described as doing sorcery (γοητείᾳ) (2.1.10.8–12). The two terms had become interchangeable by this period: Dickie, 2008, pp. 34–35.

rivals. In 8.14.1–4, he describes the tyrannical reign of the Eastern Roman Emperor Maximinus (d. ca. 313 CE). Maximinus' reign was anchored in his unparalleled esteem of sorcerers and magicians (γοήτων τε γὰρ καὶ μάγων, at 8.14.8).[206] The man was attached to idols and demons (τὰ εἴδωλα καὶ τοὺς δαίμονας, at 8.14.8).[207] In *HE* 8.14.9, Maximinus initiates a series of religious reforms: restoring divination, erecting pagan temples, rebuilding sacred groves, establishing priestly hierarchies throughout the empire, patronizing pagan cults, and appointing imperial officials (who Eusebius calls "sorcerers" [γόησιν, at 8.14.9]).[208] In Eusebius' telling of Maximinus' reign, the emperor's revitalization of Roman paganisms are guided by his love of magic. *HE* makes this demonolatrous and magical paganism an enemy of Christianity. First, it creates a conceptual overlap between paganisms and magic by implying that Maximinius' religious reforms were prompted by magic, calling Roman officials "sorcerers," correlating idol worship with demonolatry, and, finally, by framing imperial patronage of magic-laden paganism as persecution against Christians (8.14.9). *HE* also details Maximinus' shockingly depraved and violent actions against Christians (8.14.11–16). This helps advance the sorts of totalizing and reductive binaries familiar to us from contemporaneous Christian literature. The demonolatrous and evil nature of magic and heresy inflects paganisms. In contrast, only Christians are virtuous (8.14.13).

HE defends imperial orthodoxy from demonolatrous magic on all sides: from Christian heretics like Simon who wish to destroy the church from within and from non-Christians who also threaten it. Despite being besieged by demonolatrous magic-heresy since the apostolic age, though, Eusebius' story is of a victorious Christianity destined by God to conquer its enemies and reign over the empire (10.1.7–10.2.1; 10.9.9).

Looking Back from Late Antiquity

We end our literary survey with the discursive construction of imperial orthodoxy that resides at the epicenter of the Roman Empire and is therefore invested with all attendant power and privileges. Fourth-century CE authors use totalizing epistemologies to construct compelling narratives of a church triumphant. Once subject to the vagaries of empire, Christianity survived existential threats posed by demonolatrous magician-heresiarchs, real and perceived persecution, and accusations of magic directed at its wonderworking tradition – all this in addition to its conquest of its religious and epistemic rivals. Imperial orthodoxy emerges as victor over the very things that once sought its dissolution. This makes for a good story. But it is a story only possible because of the

---

[206] Greek from LCL 265, p. 304.   [207] LCL 265, p. 306.   [208] LCL 265, p. 306.

paradoxically totalizing and reductive binaries that proliferate most visibly in late ancient texts.

I think these rhetorical strategies help unpack an under-interrogated aspect of the magic-heresy conflation: How do we get to a juxtaposition between magic and truth, of all things? To ask it another way: Why does magic become the default means for delegitimating religious others? Christians were not the only ones engaged in the discursive disciplining of magic as a marker for religious deviance. However the framework for magic that coalesces in Christian texts becomes dominant, such that magic continues to be contrasted with religion even now. If we look back from late antiquity, we can see the centuries of discursive disciplining and epistemicide that resulted in this tidy formulation. The categories "magic" and "heresy" assimilated more and more epistemic terrain as they were deployed. We can also detect how said categories shifted considerably from first-century CE uses. In the New Testament, magic was the purview of ritual experts. Heresy had diffuse meanings, denoting choice or referring to factions within the earliest communities of Christ-believers. Canonical authors do not combine the two discourses, but by late antiquity, magic is heresy. It inheres in religious or epistemic others to Christianity. The fourth century's totalizing epistemologies further promote an idea of Christianity as always having been fully and essentially separate from magic-heresy. Ironically, the conceptual expansions that both categories undergo in order to be better foils for orthodoxy are also reductive. They impose a rigid interpretive binary on all religious and ritual phenomena, past to future. A given religious or epistemic system is either orthodoxy or magic-heresy. And so, we find ourselves where we started – trapped in the late ancient Christian épistémè.

Coda: Orthodoxies, Empires, and an Épistémè

"What makes orthodoxy orthodox, and how is orthodoxy violent?" asks Averil Cameron.[209] In a provocative essay, Cameron lists many of orthodoxy's violences: use of state power to compel silence or conformity; various persecutions between self-identifying Christians, but also between Christians and religious others; the creation of an "authoritarian and intolerant" discourse; and what Cameron calls the "violence of the verbal struggle," or what I call "epistemicide" throughout this Element.[210] Here, at the end of the present study, I find myself wondering if the preceding pages have been attempting to answer Cameron's question all along.

In one way, the previous sections offer an exposé of the successive cycles of discursive disciplining and epistemicide necessary for the initial erection of Christian empire. The key categories of magic and heresy became conceptual

---

[209] Cameron, 2008, p. 111. [210] Cameron, 2008, esp. pp. 112–113.

foils for imperial orthodoxy. And orthodoxy itself is evidence of violence, since it coalesces atop the dismissed religious and epistemic systems of its magical-heretical others.[211] Several forms of epistemicide haunt this study: demonizing adherents to rival systems; the invention or misrepresentation of said rivals; discrediting other leaders and experts in favor of preferred authorities; writing historiographies that center imperial orthodoxy and class all competitors as Christian heresy; claiming that Christianity was never influenced by heresy or magic; and so on. If imperial orthodoxy coalesces through iterative processes of discursive self-fashioning, then it follows that such processes create conceptual space for it by dismantling religious and epistemic competitors, including other forms of Christianity. The architects of imperial orthodoxy do more than make and mark difference through discursive disciplining and the application of pejorative labels. These writers discard what cannot be used or assimilated in order to sustain their orthodoxies.[212]

This Element, *Magic and Heresy in Ancient Christian Literature*, analyzes how magic-heresy becomes permanently fixed as conceptual demonolatrous and transgressive other to Christianity. In the introductory section, I argued that late ancient writers like Augustine create a distinctively Christian épistémè that ultimately gives the illusion of stability, of a conceptual tidiness around Christianity that crafts it as eternal, transcendent, and wholly removed from external influences like magic and heresy. Consider again Augustine's notion that all pagan gods are demonic corruptions of angels in *City of God* (12.1–6). Rival epistemic and religious systems cannot therefore be viewed as independent. Because Augustine classes them as demonic heresies, they are all folded into his totalizing épistémè. Rivals to Christianity are made comparable to it, even as they are discredited as being heretical. Epiphanius also participates in this épistémè. By locating precursors to Christian orthodoxy and heresy in the primeval past, the totalizing regime he establishes reduces all competitors to either orthodoxy or heresy (*Pan.* 1.2.7; 1.3.3). Epiphanius can thus class heresies based on proximity to his own orthodoxy. Perhaps this discursive tendency is most visible in Eusebius. *HE* sees Christianity's ascendancy as an advancement for all of humanity. Eusebius paints a picture of civilized and civilizing Christianity in contrast to barbaric paganisms (*HE* 8.14.1–17). These authors tell coherent stories that reinforce views of Christianity as fundamentally different from other epistemic and religious systems in the Roman Empire. They insist on assessing all rival systems on Christian terms.

---

[211] A point made by Jacobs, 2004, esp. pp. 1–17.
[212] On the excision of unassimilable particulars: Horkheimer and Adorno, 2002, esp. pp. 35–62.

The épistémè that coalesces in late antiquity lends itself to Western European imperial projects beyond Rome. For instance, Eusebius' *HE* contributes directly to the development of the world religions model. In his genealogy of the category of "religion," Brent Nongbri distills the creation of this model as well as its indebtedness to Christian late antiquity, and to Eusebius in particular. Eusebius does not invent the category of religion, at least not in any way approximating modern notions of it.[213] But, as Nongbri explains, "it was only the breakdown of [Eusebius'] heresiological framework in the sixteenth and seventeenth centuries that allowed the modern framework of World Religions to come into being."[214] In other words, later writers may have different intellectual projects than Eusebius, but they nevertheless replicate his logic. The heresiological framework Nongbri describes places Christianity at the center of all cosmic history and determines which of its competitors counts as proper religion by locating these traditions vis-à-vis Christianity.[215] The closer a system is to Christianity, the more legitimate it is. This is a revival of the late ancient épistémè, where writers craft totalizing frameworks that allow them to know and to classify all past and present religious and epistemic systems.

Architects of the world religions model like Marsilio Ficino did not explicitly claim non-Christian religions were heresy, but they certainly used rhetorical strategies reminiscent of someone like Eusebius. For example, Ficino believed religion was universal and that Christianity was the highest expression of it.[216] He assessed other religions based on their resemblances to Christianity. In a sense, Ficino and those of his ilk were heresiologists. Their catalogs of world religions proffered taxonomies organizing extant religions in ways strikingly similar to heresiological catalogs. Some of these catalogs even invent religions wholesale.[217] Like heresiologies, world religions catalogs ought to be read as exercises in discursive disciplining. These texts engender epistemicide while simultaneously authorizing Ficino and those like him as "knowers" of others' traditions.[218] In such catalogs, the diverse and dynamic array of world religions is reduced to commentary offered by European Christians who often did not have direct knowledge or experience of the traditions they described. Not surprising, then, that religious studies scholars have long problematized the world religions model and the field of comparative religions as being Christocentric and as extending Western European imperialism.[219]

---

[213] Nongbri, 2013, p. 57.   [214] Nongbri, 2013, p. 57.   [215] Nongbri, 2013, p. 57.
[216] Nongbri, 2013, p. 89.
[217] See Nongbri's discussion of the "religions" of India, Africa, and Japan: 2013, pp. 109–118. On Epiphanius' invention of religions: Kim, 2015, pp. 179–201; Jacobs, 2021, pp. 7–8.
[218] On "knowing" and the deconstruction of late ancient Christian empire: Jacobs, 2004, pp. 21–55.
[219] Extension of empire(s): Chidester, 1996, 2014; Christocentrism: Masuzawa, 2005, esp. pp. 12–20.

Magic-heresy is a useable discursive formation, meaning it readily lends itself to justifications of imperial conquest. Specifically, once magic is fully externalized from Christianity, it can be used as a rhetorical weapon for delegitimizing local traditions as demonic, irreligious, or inadequately religious. David Chidester relates the story of Robert Moffatt, a prominent member of the London Missionary Society. In 1842, Moffatt published an influential volume entitled *Missionary Labours and Scenes in Southern Africa*.[220] He claimed that satanism was responsible for non-Christian religions. Moffatt's missionary work, and that of his Christianizing contemporaries, is described by him as a fight against satanism.[221] Simultaneously, Moffatt claimed that Black South Africans had no religion.[222] To sustain these two contradictory claims, he used a convenient rhetorical weapon – magic. Magic had long carried connotations of satanism and corruption. When applying the label of "magic" to the non-religion of Black South Africans, Moffat claimed that they did not worship the real God, but "fetiches" and "charms."[223] This rhetorical move not only delegitimizes Black South African traditions as not properly religious, it associates them with demonolatry, thereby justifying imperialism by framing it as a holy war against the satanic.[224]

The previous examples demonstrate how magic-heresy becomes part of a larger Christian épistémè that produces useable discourses for Christian empires well beyond late antiquity. Given how effective said discourses are, is there any way to un-discipline magic-heresy, to render it less useable? I can make only gestures here, but I think we can leverage the alterity of labels like "magic" and "heresy" against the tidy and useable narratives these very categories helped forge. One method involves reclaiming magic as legitimate religious or ritual expression without recourse to negotiations of orthodoxy and heresy. An example of such an approach comes from Yvonne P. Chireau, who problematizes the application of either "religion" or "magic" to describe African American Conjure traditions.[225] She argues instead that the two are "complementary categories" referring to a complex of spiritual practices and engagement with the supernatural that can assume identifiably Christian or non-Christian forms.[226] Here, magic is not defined by its conceptual proximity to Christianity, but rather, as a means of engaging with the supernatural to effect specific, personal ends.[227] Chireau even shows how magic and Christianity are not incompatible, at least not in African American Conjure traditions.[228] In fact, reigning frameworks for magic – and religion, too – are inadequate when applied to Conjure. Instead of placing the two

---

[220] The following in Chidester, 1996, pp. 183–184. [221] Chidester, 1996, pp. 183–184.
[222] Chidester, 1996, p. 184. [223] Chidester, 1996, p. 190. [224] Chidester, 1996, p. 192.
[225] Chireau, 2006, pp. 1–9, at p. 7. [226] Chireau, 2006, p. 7. [227] Chireau, 2006, p. 3.
[228] Chireau, 2006, pp. 11–33.

in apposition, Chireau uses both together in order to highlight how Conjure draws upon, and ultimately exceeds, both magic and religion. In sum, Chireau not only complicates how scholars understand Conjure, she also troubles reigning paradigms for magic and religion.

Scholars of early Christianity, similarly, can un-discipline magic-heresy and complicate inherited narratives about Christian origins. Let me return to Origen of Alexandria's *Contra Celsum* to illustrate my point. Origen makes magic a kind of heresy by defining it as inherently demonic and immoral. Although superficial similarities may exist between miracle workers and magicians (1.68), magic can never be Christian (2.51). If we take Origen's word, then we might see magic as heretical other to his orthodoxy. This is a reasonable reading of *C. Cels.* But what if we consider this text from the perspective of our author's opponent? Can we see Origen's underlying presuppositions – the very presuppositions that eventually help produce the late ancient épistémè? I would argue that we can, certainly in *C. Cels.*, since we can read this text with Celsus. The pagan philosopher clearly did not recognize the same distinction between Christian miracle and non-Christian magic that Origen deems real and essential. Celsus seems to think that Christian wonderworkers were magicians who colluded with demons (1.6). His view is further supported by the marketplace practitioners Origen so dislikes. These individuals are not much bothered by the distinctions between magic and miracle Origen makes. Christians or not, they appeal to Jesus' name in order to effect their healings and exorcisms (1.6). So, when Origen insists that Christians solicit only the services of insider miracle workers, we can read this as a prescription against views like those espoused by Celsus. This is what Origen would like his audience to believe, but we need not take his word. Reading against the grain can expose the fact that Origen's redefinition of magic was not universal; it was a rhetorical expedient that allowed him to distance Christian miracle workers from mere magicians. Of course, it is important to note that Celsus does not offer an undistorted view of historical reality, either. Both thinkers leverage their own understandings of magic to delegitimize their religious and epistemic rival. Their differing views evidence how magic was constantly negotiated and renegotiated.

If writers like Origen create their orthodoxies in the conceptual space left by the excision of magic-heresy, then we know their creations are neither stable nor uncontested. These orthodoxies – and indeed, Christianity – must be fashioned and refashioned across cycles of discursive disciplining, through epistemicide, and sometimes, through violence at the hands of state or religious authorities. Unraveling centuries of Christian self-fashioning around the categories of magic and heresy can make us more attuned to ancient authors' assertions about the transcendence, stability, and purity of their orthodoxies. To be sure, knowing how the late ancient épistémè emerges from successive cycles of epistemicide does not erase the resultant violence, neither epistemic nor material. But exposing these discursive processes *as processes* highlights orthodoxy's ever-contested nature. In this way, we can see how Christianity, rather than being pure of magic and heresy, is profoundly indebted to both, despite ancient authors' assertions to the contrary. To recognize this is to undermine imperial legacies of Christianity as exceptional, as somehow removed from and superior to those religious and epistemic systems from which it emerged. Toward this end, I hope *Magic and Heresy* has, in a small way, aided in the disruption of the late ancient épistémè.

References

Ando, C. (2008) *The Matter of the Gods: Religion and the Roman Empire.* Princeton.

Baker-Brian, N. and Lössl, J. (eds.) (2018) *A Companion to Religion in Late Antiquity.* Malden.

Bhabha, H. K. (2004) *The Location of Culture.* Routledge Classics ed. New York.

Bonnet, M. (ed.) (1903) *Acta Apostolorum Apocrypha, Vol. 2: Acta Philippi et Acta Thomae, accedunt Acta Barabae.* Lipsiae.

Brakke, D. (2006) *Demons and the Making of the Monk: Spiritual Combat in Early Christianity.* Cambridge.

Brauner, S. (2001) *Fearless Wives and Frightened Shrews: The Construction of the Witch in Early Modern Germany.* Boston.

Bremmer, J. N. (1999) "The Birth of the Term 'Magic'," *Zeitschrift für Papyrologie und Epigraphik* 126, pp. 1–12.

Brendt, A. (2009) *Cyprian and Roman Carthage.* New York.

Broedel, H. P. (2003) *The Malleus Maleficarum and the Construction of Witchcraft: Theology and Popular Belief.* Manchester.

Buell, D. K. (1999) *Making Christians: Clement of Alexandria and the Rhetoric of Legitimacy.* Princeton.

Cain, A. (2016) *The Greek* Historia Monachorum in Aegypto: *Monastic Hagiography in the Late Fourth Century.* Oxford.

Cameron, A. (1994) *Christianity and the Rhetoric of Empire: The Development of Christian Discourse.* Berkeley.

Cameron, A. (2003) "How to Read Heresiology," *Journal of Medieval and Early Modern Studies* 33.3, pp. 471–492.

Cameron, A. (2008) "The Violence of Orthodoxy," in E. Iricinschi and H. M. Zellentin (eds.) *Heresy and Identity in Late Antiquity.* Tübingen, pp. 102–114.

Chidester, D. (1996) *Savage Systems: Colonialism and Comparative Religion in Southern Africa.* Charlottesville.

Chidester, D. (2014) *Empire of Religion: Imperialism & Comparative Religion.* Chicago.

Chireau, Y. P. (2006) *Black Magic: Religion and the African American Conjuring Tradition.* Paperback ed. Berkeley.

Clarke, G. (2008) "Christianity in the First Three Centuries: Third-Century Christianity," in A. Bowman, A. Cameron, and P. Garnsey (eds.) *The*

Cambridge Ancient History, Volume 12: The Crisis of Empire, AD 193–337. Cambridge, pp. 589–561.

Conzelmann, H. (1988) *Acts of the Apostles: A Commentary on the Acts of the Apostles*. Hermeneia: A Critical and Historical Commentary on the Bible. Minneapolis.

Coogan, M. D., Brettler, M. Z., Newsom, C. A., and Perkins, P. (eds.) (2001) *The New Oxford Annotated Bible, Third Edition*. Oxford.

Côté, D. (2001) *Le thème de l'opposition entre Pierre et Simon dans les Pseudo-Clémentines*. Paris.

Côté, D. (2012) "La forme de Dieu dans les Homélies pseudo-clémentines et la notion de Shiur Qomahm," in R. Gounelle and G. Aragione (eds.) *Soyez des changeurs avisés. Controverses exégétiques dans la littérature apocryphe chrétienne, Vol. 12*. Strasbourg, pp. 65–90.

Cotter, W. (1999) *Miracles in Graeco-Roman Antiquity: A Sourcebook for the Study of New Testament Miracle Stories*. New York.

Dickie, M. W. (2008) *Magic and Magicians in the Greco-Roman World*. New York.

Dombrowski, P. J. (2018) "The Invention of Magic in the Age of Augustus," PhD diss. University of North Carolina.

Dunn, G. D. (2004a) "Heresy and Schism according to Cyprian of Carthage," *Journal of Theological Studies* 55.2, pp. 551–574.

Dunn, G. D. (2004b) *Tertullian*. New York.

Dyson, R. W. (ed. & trans.) (1998) *Augustine*, The City of God against the Pagans. New York.

Edmonds III, R. G. (2019) *Drawing Down the Moon: Magic in the Ancient Greco-Roman World*. Princeton.

Ehrman, B. D. (ed. & trans.) (2003a) *The Apostolic Fathers, Volume I: I Clement. II Clement. Ignatius. Polycarp. Didache*. LCL 24. Cambridge.

Ehrman, B. D. (ed. & trans.) (2003b) *The Apostolic Fathers, Volume II: Epistle of Barnabas. Papias and Quadratus. Epistle to Diognetus. The Shepherd of Hermas*. LCL 25. Cambridge.

Elliott, J. K. (1993) *The Apocryphal New Testament: A Collection of Apocryphal Christian Literature in an English Translation Based on M.R. James*. Oxford.

Eshleman, K. (2012) *The Social World of Intellectuals in the Roman Empire: Sophists, Philosophers, and Christians*. Cambridge.

Evans, E. (ed. & trans.) (1948) *Tertullian's Treatise against Praxeas*. London.

Fitzmyer, J. (1988) *The Acts of the Apostles*. Anchor Bible Commentaries. New York.

Flint, V. (1999) "The Demonisation of Magic and Sorcery in Late Antiquity: Christian Redefinitions of Pagan Religions," in V. Flint, R. Gordon, G. Luck, and D. Ogden (eds.) *Witchcraft and Magic in Europe, Volume 2: Ancient Greece and Rome*. London, pp. 277–348.

Flower, R. (2010) "Genealogies of Unbelief: Epiphanius of Salamis and Heresiological Authority," in C. Kelly, R. Flower, and M. S. Williams (eds.) *Unclassical Traditions: Volume II: Perspectives from the East and West in Late Antiquity*. Cambridge, pp. 70–87.

Foucault, M. (1970) *The Order of Things: An Archaeology of the Human Sciences*. Pantheon Books.

Frankfurter, D. (ed.) (2019) *Guide to the Study of Ancient Magic*. Leiden.

Gallagher, E. V. (1982) *Divine Man or Magician? Celsus and Origen on Jesus*. Chico.

Garnsey, P. and Humphress, P. C. (2001) *The Evolution of the Late Antique World*. Cambridge.

Garrett, S. R. (1989) *The Demise of the Devil: Magic and the Demonic in Luke's Writings*. Minneapolis.

Gordon, R. (1999) "Imagining Greek and Roman Magic," in V. Flint, R. Gordon, G. Luck, and D. Ogden (eds.) *Witchcraft and Magic in Europe, Volume 2: Ancient Greece and Rome*. London, pp. 159–276.

Graf, F. (1997) *Magic in the Ancient World*. F. Philip (trans.). Cambridge.

Haar, S. (2003) *Simon Magus: The First Gnostic?* Berlin.

Han, J. H. (2023) *Prophets and Prophecy in the Late Antique Near East*. New York.

Harkins, P. W. (trans.) (1979) *St. John Chrysostom: Discourses against Judaizing Christians*. New York.

Holl, K. (ed.) (1915) *Die griechischedn christlichen Schriftstellen der ersten drei Jahrhunderte: Epiphanius, erster Band: Anchoratus und Panarion Haer. 1–33*. Leipzig.

Holmén, T. (2007) "Jesus and Magic: Theodicean Perspectives to the Issue," in M. Labahn and B. J. L. Peerbolte (eds.) *A Kind of Magic: Understanding Magic in the New Testament and Its Religious Environment*. New York, pp. 43–56.

Horkheimer, M. and Adorno, T. W. (2002) *Dialectic of Enlightenment*. E. Jephcott (trans.) and G. S. Noerr (ed.). Stanford.

Jacobs, A. S. (2004) *Remains of the Jews: The Holy Land and Christian Empire in Late Antiquity*. Stanford.

Jacobs, A. S. (2021) *Epiphanius of Cyprus: A Cultural Biography of Late Antiquity*. Berkeley.

Janowitz, N. (2001) *Magic in the Roman World: Pagans, Jews, and Christians*. London.

Kahlos, M. (2015) "*Artis Heu Magicis*: The Label of Magic in Fourth-Century Conflicts and Disputes," in M. R. Salzman, M. Sághy, and R. L. Testa (eds.) *Pagans and Christians in Late Antique Rome*. Cambridge, pp. 162–177.

Kahlos, M. (2019) *Religious Dissent in Late Antiquity, 350–450*. Oxford.

Kahlos, M. (2020) "A Christian Cannot Employ Magic: Rhetorical Sefl-Fashioning and the Magicless Christianity of Late Antiquity," in R. Flower and M. Ludlow (eds.) *Rhetoric and Religious Identity in Late Antiquity*. Oxford, pp. 128–142.

Kelley, N. (2006) *Knowledge and Religious Authority in the Pseudo-Clementines*. Tübingen.

Kim, Y. R. (2006) "The Imagined Worlds of Epiphanius of Cyprus," Ph.D. diss. University of Michigan.

Kim, Y. R. (2015) *Epiphanius of Cyprus: Imagining an Orthodox World*. Ann Arbor.

Klauck, H.-J. (2003) *Magic and Paganism in Early Christianity: The World of the Acts of the Apostles*. B. McNeill (trans.). Minneapolis.

Klutz, T. (2003) "Reinterpreting 'Magic' in the World of Jewish and Christian Scripture," in T. Klutz (ed.) *Magic in the Biblical World: From the Rod of Aaron to the Ring of Solomon*. London, pp. 1–11.

Koester, C. R. (2003) *Symbolism in the Fourth Gospel: Meaning, Mystery, Community*. Augsburg.

Koetschau, P. (ed.) (1899a) *Die griechischedn christlichen Schriftstellen der ersten drei Jahrhunderte: Origenes, erster Band: Die Schrift vom Martyrium; Buch I-IV gegen Celsus*. Leipzig.

Koetschau, P. (ed.) (1899b) *Die griechischedn christlichen Schriftstellen der ersten drei Jahrhunderte: Origenes, zweiter Band: Buch V-VIII gegen Celsus; Die Schrift vom Gebet*. Leipzig.

Lake, K. (ed. & trans.) (1926) *Eusebius: The Ecclesiastical History: Volume 1*. LCL 153. Cambridge.

Lampinen, A. (2022) "'Ethnic' Divination in Roman Imperial Literature," in C. Addey (ed.) *Divination and Knowledge in Greco-Roman Antiquity*. New York, pp. 218–247.

Le Boulluec, A. (2022) *The Notion of Heresy in Greek Literature in the Second and Third Centuries*. A. K. M. Adam, M. Cuany, N. Moore, W. Campbell, with J. Wood (trans.). Oxford.

Litwa, M. D. (ed. & trans.) (2016) *The Refutation of All Heresies*. Atlanta.

Lookadoo, J. (2023) *The Christology of Ignatius of Antioch*. Eugene.

Loriot, X. and Nony, D. (1997) *La crise de l'empire romain, 235–284*. Paris.

MacMullen, R. (1984) *Christianizing the Roman Empire (A.D. 100–400)*. New Haven.

Masuzawa, T. (2005) *The Invention of World Religions: Or, How European Universalism Was Preserved in the Language of Pluralism*. Chicago.

Mitchell, M. M. (2022) "John Chrysostom and Christian Love Magic: A Spellbinding Moment in the History of Interpretation of 1 Cor 7.2–4," *New Testament Studies* 68, pp. 119–143.

Moss, C. R. (2010) *The Other Christs: Imitating Jesus in Ancient Christian Ideologies of Martyrdom*. Oxford.

Moss, C. R. (2012) *Ancient Christian Martyrdom: Diverse Practices, Theologies, and Traditions*. New Haven.

Nasrallah, L. (2003) *An Ecstasy of Folly: Prophecy and Authority in Early Christianity*. Cambridge.

Nongbri, B. (2013) *Before Religion: A History of a Modern Concept*. New Haven.

Padilla Peralta, D. (2020) "Epistemicide: The Roman Case," *Classica* 33, pp. 151–186.

Patel, S. S. (2021) "Notes on Rehabilitating 'Magic' in the Study Early Christian Literature," *Religion Compass* 15, pp. 1–10.

Patel, S. S. (2025) *Smoke & Mirrors: Discourses of Magic in Early Petrine Traditions*. New York.

Porter, S. F. (2007) "Magic in the Book of Acts," in M. Labahn and B. J. L. Peerbolte (eds.) *A Kind of Magic: Understanding Magic in the New Testament and Its Religious Environment*. New York, pp. 107–121.

Proctor, T. W. (2022) *Demonic Bodies and the Dark Ecologies of Early Christian Culture*. New York.

Reed, A. Y. (2003) "'Jewish Christianity' after the 'Parting of the Ways': Approaches to Historiography and Self-Definition in the Pseudo-Clementine Literature," in A. H. Becker and A. Y. Reed (eds.) *The Ways that Never Parted: Jews and Christians in Late Antiquity and the Early Middle Ages*. Tübingen, pp. 197–231.

Reed, A. Y. (2004) "The Trickery of the Fallen Angels and the Demonic Mimesis of the Divine: Aetiology, Demonology, and Polemics in the Writings of Justin Martyr," *Journal of Early Christian Studies* 12.2, pp. 141–171.

Reed, A. Y. (2008) "Heresiology and the (Jewish-)Christian Novel: Narrativized Polemics in the Pseudo-Clementines," in E. Iricinschi and H. M. Zellentin (eds.) *Heresy and Self-Definition in Late Antiquity*. Tübingen, pp. 273–298.

Reed, A. Y. (2009) "Jewish Christianity as Counter-History? The Apostolic Past in Eusebius' *Ecclesiastical History* and the Pseudo-Clementine *Homilies*," in G. Gardner and K. Osterloh (eds.) *Antiquity in Antiquity: Jewish and Christian Pasts in the Greco-Roman World*. Tübingen, pp. 173–216.

Reed, A. Y. (2014) "Gendering Heavenly Secrets? Women Angels, and the Problem of Misogyny and Magic," in K. B. Stratton and D. S. Kalleres (eds.) *Daughters of Hecate: Women and Magic in the Ancient World*. New York, pp. 108–151.

Ricks, S. D. (1995) "The Magician as Outsider in the Hebrew Bible and the New Testament," in M. Meyer and P. Mirecki (eds.) *Ancient Magic and Ritual Power*. Leiden, pp. 131–143.

Rives, J. B. (1999) "The Decree of Decius and the Religion of Empire," *Journal of Roman Studies* 89, pp. 135–157.

Rives, J. B. (2003) "Magic in Roman Law: The Reconstruction of a Crime," *Classical Antiquity* 22.2, pp. 313–339.

Royalty Jr., R. M. (2015) *The Origin of Heresy: A History of Discourse in Second Temple Judaism and Early Christianity*. Reprint. New York.

Sanzo, J. E. (2019) "Early Christianity," in D. Frankfurter (ed.) *Guide to the Study of Early Magic*. Leiden, pp. 198–239.

Schneemelcher, W. S. (2003) *New Testament Apocrypha Vol. 2*. Revised ed. R. M. Wilson (ed. & trans.). Louisville.

Schott, J. (2007) "Heresiology as Universal History in Epiphanius's *Panarion*," *Zeitschrift für Antikes Christentum* 10, pp. 546–563.

Schroeder, C. T. (2007) *Monastic Bodies: Discipline and Salvation in Shenoute of Atripe*. Philadelphia.

Simon, M. (1979) "From Greek Hairesis to Christian Heresy," in W. R. Schoedel and R. L. Wilken (eds.) *Early Christian Literature and the Classical Intellectual Tradition: In Honorem Robert M. Grant*. Paris, pp. 101–116.

Slootjes, D. (2011) "Bishops and Their Power in the Late Third Century: The Cases of Gregory Thaumaturgus and Paul of Samosata," *Journal of Late Antiquity* 4.1, pp. 100–115.

Smith, G. S. (2014) *Guilt by Association: Heresy Catalogues in Early Christianity*. New York.

Soon, I. T. (2021) "Disability and New Testament Studies: Reflections, Trajectories, and Possibilities," *Journal of Disability and Religion* 25.4, pp. 374–387.

de Sousa Santos, B. (2014) "Epistemologies of the South and the Future," *From the European South* 1, pp. 17–29.

Stenschke, C. W. (1999) *Luke's Portrait of Gentiles Prior to Their Coming to Faith*. Tübingen.

Stephens, W. (2020) "'In the Body': The *Canon Episcopi*, Andrea Alciati, and Gianfrancesco Piso's Humanized Demons," in J. Goodacre, R. Voltmer, and L. H. Willumsen (eds.) *Demonology and Witch-Hunting in Early Modern Europe*. New York, pp. 86–106.

Stratton, K. B. (2007) *Naming the Witch: Magic, Ideology, and Stereotype in the Ancient World*. New York.

Stratton, K. B. and Kalleres, D. S. (eds.) (2014) *Daughters of Hecate: Women and Magic in the Ancient World*. New York.

Styers, R. (2008) *Making Magic: Religion, Magic, and Science in the Modern World*. New York.

Tupamahu, E. (2022) *Contesting Languages: Heteroglossia and the Politics of Language in the Early Church*. New York.

Twelftree, G. H. (2007) *In the Name of Jesus: Exorcism among the Early Christians*. Grand Rapids.

Twelftree, G. H. (2020) "Jesus, Magician or Miracle Worker?" *Biblical Annals* 10.3, pp. 405–436.

Vanden Eykel, E. (2022) *The Magi: Who They Were, How They've Been Remembered, and Why They Still Fascinate*. Minneapolis.

Watts, E. J. (2021) *The Eternal Decline and Fall of Rome: The History of Dangerous Idea*. New York.

Weingarten, S. (2005) *The Saint's Saints: Hagiography and Geography in Jerome*. Leiden.

Wendt, H. (2016) *At the Temple Gates: The Religion of Freelance Experts in the Roman Empire*. New York.

Witmer, A. (2012) *Jesus, the Galilean Exorcist: His Exorcisms in Social and Political Context*. New York.

Ziolkowski, A. (2011) "The Background to the Third-Century Crisis of the Roman Empire," in K. A. Raaflaub and J. P. Árnason (eds.) *The Roman Empire in Context: Historical and Comparative Perspectives*. Malden, pp. 111–133.

Acknowledgments

This Element would not have been written without the support and editorial guidance of Andrew S. Jacobs. When Andrew approached me to write it, I had not finished revising my first monograph. Still, he saw something worthwhile in my early articulations about the discursive formation of ancient magic and heresy and he gave me the freedom to experiment. I did not make his editorial duties easy, I'm afraid. But Andrew is the very best of us, and he saw this project through many and various difficulties. I am thankful for all his support. *Magic and Heresy* is also deeply indebted to my conversations with Ananda Abeysekara, a brilliant scholar of Buddhist Studies who identified Asad as a kind of methodological lode star. The genealogical structure of this Element is resultant of Ananda's influence, though admittedly, I could never achieve the sharpness of either Asad or Abeysekara. Toward the end, I was, as ever, reliant on Jason Robert Combs. Jason is a thoughtful and incisive reader, and his suggestions for revision helped clarify an argumentative throughline. More than that, though, Jason is a long-time friend and a trusted interlocutor who never laughs at my ideas, though I think he probably should. At least at some of them.

There are many others who supported me and this project, from its inception to its submission. Ellen Muehlberger invited me to give the lecture that sparked this inquiry. I am particularly thankful to Bart Ehrman, Jeremiah Coogan, and Meghan Henning for talking through some of my major points. Young Richard Kim's welcome among "Epiphaniacs" was a much-needed kindness in tough times. Ipsita Chatterjea prompted me to think about *Magic and Heresy*'s implications for Religious Studies more broadly. Todd Berzon reviewed the original MS for CUP; his meticulous and incisive comments helped make it clearer, and better. I am likewise thankful to a second, anonymous reviewer who also offered meaningful feedback. I hope this project is much stronger than its earlier iterations. Its remaining deficiencies are, of course, attributable to me as author.

I am sure I have forgotten others – a great many others – who helped shape this Element. My forgetfulness should not diminish their contributions. No one writes anything alone. So, I thank the scores of interlocutors I have had over the last several years. I am a better thinker now than I was when I graduated from my PhD program. I am a better person, too. I credit that to family, friends, and colleagues who so generously shared their time and energy. In the same spirit, I thank my reader, for sharing your time and energy, too. I hope *Magic and Heresy* offers something useful for your own thinking around magic and heresy, empire and epistemicide.

To Bapuji, in gratitude

Cambridge Elements

Religion in Late Antiquity

Andrew S. Jacobs
Harvard Divinity School

Andrew S. Jacobs is Senior Fellow at the Center for the Study of World Religions at Harvard Divinity School. He has taught at the University of California, Riverside, Scripps College, and Harvard Divinity School and is the author of *Remains of the Jews: The Holy Land and Christian Empire in Late Antiquity; Christ Circumcised: A Study in Early Christian History and Difference;* and *Epiphanius of Cyprus: A Cultural Biography of Late Antiquity.* He has co-edited *Christianity in Late Antiquity, 300–450 C.E.: A Reader* and *Garb of Being: Embodiment and the Pursuit of Asceticism in Late Ancient Christianity.*

Editorial Board
Krista Dalton, *Kenyon College*
Heidi Marx, *University of Manitoba*
Ellen Muehlberger, *University of Michigan*
Michael Pregill, *Los Angeles, California*
Kristina Sessa, *Ohio State University*
Stephen J. Shoemaker, *University of Oregon*

About the Series
This series brings a holistic and comparative approach to religious belief and practice from 100–800 C.E. throughout the Mediterranean and Near East. Volumes will explore the key themes that characterize religion in late antiquity and will often cross traditional disciplinary lines. The series will include contributions from classical studies, Early Christianity, Judaism, and Islam, among other fields.

Cambridge Elements

Religion in Late Antiquity

Elements in the Series

Theory, History, and the Study of Religion in Late Antiquity: Speculative Worlds
Maia Kotrosits

Monasticism and the City in Late Antiquity and the Early Middle Ages
Mateusz Fafinski and Jakob Riemenschneider

Israel and its Heirs in Late Antiquity
Andrew Tobolowsky

Magic and Heresy in Ancient Christian Literature
Shaily Shashikant Patel

A full series listing is available at: www.cambridge.org/ELAN

Printed by Libri Plureos GmbH in Hamburg, Germany